D0805536

ENDING
WORLD HUNGER

ENDING WORLD HUNGER

BY NATHAN AASENG

A Science/Technology/Society Book
Series Consultant: Charles R. Barman
FRANKLIN WATTS
New York/London/Toronto/Sydney
1991

To Bessie Olson, in greatest
admiration for her efforts

Photographs courtesy of: United Nations: pp. 14 (FAO), 17, 30 (Peter Magubane), 62 bottom (A. Holcombe), 120 (John Isaac), 126 (FAO/F. Botts); Gamma-Liaison: pp. 20 top (Phillip Parker), 20 bottom (Alan Weiner), 50 (Claes Lofgren); U.S. Department of Agriculture: pp. 62 top, 78; Texas A&M University: p. 66; Impact Visuals: p. 70 (Rick Gerharter); Granada Bio-Sciences, Inc.: p. 98; Sovfoto/Eastfoto: p. 113 (Wu Yuanliu).

Library of Congress Cataloging-in-Publication Data

Aaseng, Nathan.
    Ending world hunger / by Nathan Aaseng.
      p.   cm. — (A Science/technology/society book)
    Includes bibliographical references and index.
    Summary: Studies the political, social, and scientific-technical reasons for world food shortages, and focuses on possible approaches to increasing food production.
    ISBN 0-531-11007-9
    1. Food supply. 2. Famines. 3. Hunger. 4. Poverty. 5. Food relief. 6. Produce trade—Government policy. [1. Food supply. 2. Famines. 3. Hunger.] I. Title. II. Series.
HD9000.5.A18   1991
363.8—dc20   90-46207 CIP AC

CONTENTS

INTRODUCTION

HUNGER IN A WORLD OF PLENTY

Mealtime. For some it means choosing from among twelve pages of fabulous entrées at a posh restaurant. For some it means peeking in the oven to see what is creating that delicious aroma. For some it is sitting down to a small portion of the usual rice and vegetables.

For some it is a dream that will never come true.

Hunger is the most basic of human problems. The fact that it is so widespread today is perhaps the most searing indictment of modern society. While consumers in industrialized societies gorge themselves on the raw materials of the world to meet their ever-mounting demands for comfort and convenience, children die for lack of food.

The evidence is available as never before from all corners of the world. Reams of statistics have been churned out to measure the level of hunger in the world. At least 700 million of the world's 5 billion people suffer from a serious shortage of food.[1] Probably twice that many lack the proper amount of protein and number of calories in their diet to lead a normal, active life.[2]

Roughly 15 to 20 million people will die this year from starvation, and perhaps 20 million more will die from diseases caused or aggravated by lack of food.[3] Hunger is most destructive for the most helpless members of society—the aged, the crippled, abandoned women, and especially children. It is estimated that one of every four children in the world is always hungry. Nearly 15 million children under the age of five die each year from famine and the resulting diseases.[4] That breaks down to 1 million per month, or 40,000 children every day. In some areas of the world half of the children die of hunger-related causes.

Even those who escape death often carry the scars of hunger for the rest of their lives. The number of people whose bodies have been stunted or whose brains have been damaged by malnutrition has been estimated at a billion.

But statistics, however staggering, do not tell the story of hunger. Photographs and television pictures are better suited for that task. They capture the haunting images of emaciated bodies, large, glassy eyes staring out of fleshless faces, necks too weak to support heads. Each one of these images represents more than a statistic. He or she is a person—someone's son or daughter. If even one parent in this world has to go to bed at night listening to the sound of his or her child whimpering for food, it is a tragedy almost beyond bearing.

The cruelest part of the situation is that every one of those hungry stomachs could have been filled in the past decades, every one of these tragedies prevented. Despite the ravages of nature in recent years, the world has produced enough food on average to provide every person on the planet with an adequate diet. Yet we still cannot feed our hungry.

While this brings down a heavy load of guilt on our present societies, it puts an even more ominous burden on our future. The bottom line is that there are more hungry people in the world at this moment than ever before, and the number is growing. If we cannot feed the hungry now, in a world of plenty, what will happen in years to come when the twin problems of environmental deterioration and rapidly expanding population put a greater strain on our ability to feed the world? How long can we continue to wring greater supplies of food from our earth before we reach the limits of its resources?

CHAPTER 1
HUNGER IN A
WORLD OF LIMITS

During the 1960s and 1970s, world agricultural production grew at about 3 percent a year.[5] These gains were more than enough to offset a large increase in population during that time. But according to the 1988 Report of the United Nations Food Council, the progress made during the 1970s in the battle against hunger has come to a halt.[6] In many parts of the world the situation is growing worse instead of better.

WORLD FOOD SUPPLY

At the beginning of the 1987 harvest, grain was so plentiful in the world that United States farmers were encouraged to take land out of production to ease the glut. World food production had sailed along on a pattern of nonstop growth ever since the World War II recovery period in the late 1940s. Storage facilities were filled with 459 metric tons of surplus grain. The unused grain was enough to feed the world for 101 days.[7]

The seeming invincibility of modern agriculture was shattered, however, by a series of natural disasters. In 1987 India's monsoon rains failed to appear. The following year a devastating drought parched the grain belts of North America and China. North American grain production plunged by 25 percent. The Chinese harvest was down by at least 10 percent, and the Soviet Union also showed a moderate decline.[8]

Suddenly, after nearly four decades of continuous growth, world harvests experienced steep declines two years in a row. In just two years, the world's grain reserves plunged from the highest level ever to the lowest level since the early 1970s. At the beginning of the 1989 harvest, world grain stocks were adequate to supply only sixty days of food for the world.[9]

Meanwhile, Third World countries were falling behind in their efforts to grow their own food. Twenty years ago, Africa was not only self-supporting in terms of food but actually exported more food than it imported. In the 1970s, however, Africa became the first continent in modern times to lose ground in the war against hunger. Since 1967 African grain production per person has dropped by 15 percent.[10]

In the 1980s, Latin America became the next major region to fall behind in production. Since 1981, Latin America's per capita grain production has declined almost as much as Africa's.[11]

SOIL

The soil that has provided the nourishment for human life throughout history is not a limitless food-growing factory. Rather it is a relatively scarce resource. About 75 percent of the earth's surface is covered with water. Of the remaining 25 percent, a fifth is located in climates that are too cold to grow food. Another fifth lies in climates too dry to support food production, and another fifth is made up of mountains and other areas too rugged to farm. That leaves a total of about 10 percent of the earth's surface on which food may be grown, and that includes fragile land that can support minimal amounts of crops.

Yet this limited resource is often treated as though it were expendable. An alarming amount of that precious 10 percent is being destroyed every year by construction, erosion, desertification, and overgrazing.

Urban and suburban development paves over much quality farmland. During the 1970s the Japanese lost 7 percent of their cropland to the encroachment of civilization.[12] China has lost 13 percent of its crop-growing area since 1976, primarily to homes and factories. Urban construction over the past decade has claimed 29 million acres of cropland in the United States.[13]

As the rural populations of the world continue to flock toward large cities, this demand for urban living space will increase. It is projected that at current rates there will be twenty Third World cities with populations of 30 million by the year 2050.[14] The housing, industry, and transportation systems needed to support such populations will require a great deal of additional land. Unfortunately, the most desirable land on which to live is frequently prime farmland.

The farmland that escapes the concrete coating of urban progress can continue to supply food only because it contains a thin life-support system known as topsoil. These few inches of topsoil provide the nutrients necessary for the growth of edible plants. Again, this precious resource is being squandered at alarming rates. Modern, industrial farming, in which land is cleared and planted with a single, profitable species of grain, has contributed to this erosion. Billions of tons of topsoil are blown away by winds or washed into the sea every year. As a result, much farmland is losing its fertility—its ability to support plants.[15]

This vital link to life cannot be easily replaced. Depending on the climatic conditions, it takes from 100 to 400 years to generate a single centimeter of topsoil.[16]

While choice farmland is disappearing, the wastelands of the earth are growing. On every continent, deserts are expanding, eating up once-productive land. The Sahara Desert, much of which was farmed in ancient times, has been creeping steadily southward, enveloping thousands of villages.[17] Much of this desertification is caused by large herds of domestic animals stripping the limited plant growth of marginal rangelands. Until the 1950s, the semiarid border of the Sahara known as the Sahel supported the flocks of nomadic herdsmen. These people followed the rains north during the wet season and moved to the wetter land of the south during the dry season. A small number of crops were planted, with the ground allowed to lie fallow for long periods to replenish itself between crops.

During the 1950s and 1960s, however, governments placed restrictions on the movement of nomads who had never paid attention to the bound-

Skull of a cow is all that remains of what
was once a pasture full of grazing cattle
in the Sahelian Zone of Africa. This region
on the southern edge of the Sahara Desert,
comprising the nations of Mauritania,
Mali, Senegal, Burkina Faso, Niger,
and Chad, has seen a slow process of
desertification in the last thirty years.

aries drawn up by politicians. Forced to remain in one spot, the nomads had to plant more crops that depleted the thin soil. Their livestock began to eat away and trample the vegetation. Trees were chopped down to provide firewood.

Now, once-green lands lie under mountains of sand, never to be green again. Grit and dust hang in the air. Women may spend half a day searching for the wood to cook their meals.

The Soviet Union attempted to expand its grain production into dry, minimally productive regions during the 1970s. Initially the results were favorable as more land was brought into production. But the expansion upset the fragile ecological balance of those areas. Laid open to the effects of wind and erosion, the land lost its ability to support life. After losing 250,000 acres of cropland a year to erosion, the Soviet Union now has far less available cropland than it had twenty years ago.[18] More than a third of India's fertile lands has been damaged by overgrazing and the loss of forest cover.[19] Altogether, it is estimated that 25,000 square miles of the world's arable land are turned to desert each year because of human misuse.[20]

The removal of trees in the lush rain forests of the tropics has spawned its own unique form of desertification. Rain forests do not accumulate nutrients in the soil, as do lands in more temperate climates. Rather, they store them in living matter. The heat and humidity decays dead plant material so quickly that nutrients can be quickly converted to use by living plants. When rain forests are cleared away for agriculture, the nutrients are cleared away along with the trees. The land that remains can support plant growth for a few years at best. After that, the sun bakes it into a hard, sterile crust.[21] It takes only a few years for some of the most diverse and rapidly growing plant communities to convert to veritable deserts. Since 1960 two-thirds of the productive rain forests in the Ivory Coast have been removed.[22] At the present rate of destruction, Brazil's lush rain forests will be gone in thirty-five years. In their place, we find barren ground.

Little unused cropland is available to replace the productive land that is being sterilized. The United States could reactivate farmland taken out of production due to past grain gluts, amounting to about 2 percent of the world's total cropland.[23] Latin America and Africa still have untapped areas that could be put into production. But, worldwide, if all unused arable land were cultivated, the total cropland would increase by only about 10 percent. When we look for ways to add to the world's food supply, we shall have to look somewhere other than to unused land.

WATER

Many experts believe that world food production will ultimately be limited as much by the scarcity of the water supply as by the limits of cropland. Water shortages have already developed in many of the drier, heavily populated areas, such as the Southwestern United States.

Water reserves and their limitations can be described in two ways: fossil water and water tables. Fossil water comes from underground reservoirs that do not have sources of replenishment. Once they are drained, they are gone forever. Those crops irrigated by fossil water offer no food security. In fact, the use of such water amounts to nothing more

A sign posted in the Amazon rain forest reads, in Portuguese, "Preserve the Green." During the past several decades, the world's tropical rain forests have been cut down at an alarming rate. Often the farmland created can only be cultivated for a few years before it loses the nutrients required to sustain crops.

than feeding today's people at the expense of the future.

Water tables are made up of underground water that can be replaced by rainwater. Yet there is a limit to how much of this can be replaced. Many areas are already draining their water tables because of their current food production efforts. The water table in the North China plain, for example, has been dropping three feet per year. Such a drain cannot be supported indefinitely.[24]

The Soviet Union has recently provided stark evidence of the disastrous effects of siphoning water from rivers and inland seas for irrigation.[25] In 1918 the Soviet government initiated a plan to increase cotton production in the dry lands around the Aral Sea. Two major rivers, the Amu Darya and the Syr Darya, were tapped to support these new fields. In 1954 the huge Kara Kum Canal was dug to divert even more water to the cotton, melon, and grain fields. Eventually 18 million acres were irrigated by water from these rivers.

This demand proved to be far more than the rivers could support. Both rivers slowed to a trickle and frequently dried up altogether before reaching the Aral Sea. The 26,000-square-mile (67,000-sq-km) Aral Sea, the fourth-largest inland body of water in the world, began to shrink. By 1990 it had lost 40 percent of its surface area. More than 11,000 square miles (28,000 sq km) of water had been turned into a salt desert.

The town of Muynuk once rested on the shores of the Aral Sea. Its people made their living primarily by fishing, catching about 3 percent of the Soviet Union's annual fish harvest. In just twenty-five years, the Aral Sea has evaporated so much that Muynuk now lies stranded at least 20 miles from the water. Even if the 10,000 fishermen of Muynuk were able to gain access to the sea, there are no commercial fish left. The concentration of salt caused by the evaporation of the water has killed off all native species. At its current rate of disappearance, the Aral Sea will lose yet another third of its area by the year 2000.

The United States, too, has experienced alarming drops in fresh water levels. About a quarter of the crops irrigated in the United States are watered by drawing down the water table.[26] Since 1941, the metropolitan area of Los Angeles has filled 15 percent of its water needs by diverting streams that feed Mono Lake.[27] After water levels in that lake plunged by more than 40 feet, a judge ordered the city to limit its use of this source. During the drought of 1988 the mighty Mississippi River declined to its lowest level on record.[28]

The oceans that cover so much of the earth would seem to be a prime source for additional food. After all, 80 percent of the world's creatures live in the sea. Presently, humans harvest only a tiny percentage of their calories and protein from this enormous habitat.[29] But the fact is that some parts of the oceans have already been overfished. Many of the most desirable species are declining in number. Fewer pounds of fish are pulled from the seas today than were harvested twenty years ago.[30] Monterey Bay in California, for example, once supported a robust sardine industry. Overfishing wiped out the sardine population, and this industry went out of business shortly after World War II.[31]

ENVIRONMENTAL LIMITS

Much of the increase in world food production has been due to the introduction of industrial methods of farming.[32] Unfortunately, industry and nature have not been the best of partners, and industrial farming has been no exception. Almost all of the increase in food production in the twentieth century has come from practices that put a severe strain on the environment.

It has been estimated that the use of chemical fertilizers alone is counted upon to produce the food that nourishes a billion and a half people.[33] The processing of these fertilizers involves large quantities of chemical raw materials and consumes a great deal of energy. Further, by-products of the fertilizer-making process concentrate in ground water, making it unsafe to drink. These by-products feed the formation of algae blooms that choke the life out of lakes and streams.

More than 45,000 different poison products,[34] employing more than 600 different active ingredients, are sprayed onto fields to eliminate weeds and control pests. Many of these poisons linger in

Top: Barges stuck in the Mississippi River during the drought of 1988, when the river fell to its lowest level on record. *Bottom:* Crops in Georgia withered by drought.

the air and soil for years. The vast cotton fields of the southern Soviet Union have been so saturated with pesticides over the past few decades that much of the land is unfit to grow anything else.[35] United States farmers alone dump several billion pounds of poisons into the environment each year. The United States Environmental Protection Agency considers this enormous pesticide use to be the country's most serious environmental problem.[36]

Although pesticides have been products of industrialized nations, they may do even more damage to Third World nations. Poisons too toxic to be cleared for use in the United States may be exported to poorer countries where government funds are not available for setting or enforcing standards of toxicity.[37]

The conversion of forests to cropland, mentioned previously, is an invitation for environmental disaster quite apart from loss of soil. The stripping of forests in India and Nepal left the land without enough vegetation to soak up heavy monsoon rains in the mid-1980s. The result was flooding further downstream in the Bangladesh lowlands that left millions homeless.[38]

Another serious environmental problem introduced by modern farming techniques is the "monoculture." By far the most efficient means of food production is to plant a single crop in a large field. This uniformity makes it easy to plant, tend, and harvest with large machines. But, again, human efficiency runs squarely against the grain of nature. Diverse horticultural communities are far better equipped for survival than are single-plant communities. This is because different plants use different nutrients. Between them they can make use of all the nutrients in the soil without exhausting any one of them. Monocultures suck the soil dry of those nutrients they require.[39]

A complex community is also far more able to survive disaster. It can bounce back quickly from both droughts and floods because it contains members that can tolerate a variety of conditions. Monocultures live or die according to the weather. Insects and other pests develop very specific means of defeating the defenses of the plant species they attack. What works against one plant does not necessarily work against another. If a new pest invades a diverse community, therefore, its effect is limited. It can destroy only a small portion of the plant life. But an invasion of insects or bacteria can easily wipe out an entire monoculture community.

Finally, the environmental problem of global warming may have serious implications for the farming community. The so-called "greenhouse" effect comes from the growing amount of carbon dioxide in the atmosphere caused by the burning of fossil fuels. An increase of just a few degrees Fahrenheit in the world's average temperature could trigger catastrophic changes in climate. The best estimates predict that two of the major food-producing regions of the world, the North American Plains and central Asia, would be greatly affected.[40] Both areas would probably become too hot and dry to support their present massive food production.

All of these factors cast a shadow on the future of food production. The world's resources for producing traditional crops are limited. There are also limits to how much punishment we can inflict on our environment with our food-production methods. Whether or not we are reaching those limits is a subject for study and debate. What is not debatable is that the demand for food will increase in the years to come as the world's population grows.

POPULATION

If the world is unable to feed its current population, despite taking dangerous chances with the environment in its attempt to do so, any additional demand for food poses a serious problem. With the current rate of population growth, that additional demand will be severe.

The world population is growing at the rate of a little over 2 percent each year.[41] That may seem insignificant, but it results in doubling of the population every forty years. This means that the world will have to produce twice as much food as is grown now just to keep hunger at its present intolerable level. Some countries are facing growth rates of between 3 and 4 percent, which means a doubling time of only twenty-four years.

If present rates were to continue, there would be 30 billion humans on the earth by the year 2075, six mouths to feed for every person currently alive. Population growth rates are slowing and are likely to continue to do so. But the momentum built up by decades of rapid growth guarantees hefty increases for the next half century. The population boom has already produced billions of children who will one day have children of their own. So even if the birth rate were immediately reduced to two children per couple, the population would continue to increase until the present generation of children has had its children.

World population will almost certainly climb to six billion by the turn of the century, one billion more than present figures. Most experts estimate that several billion more people will be added before the situation stabilizes. During the next half century or so, world food production may well have to increase by as much as it has since the first seed was sown by human hands![42] Most disheartening of all is that nine out of every ten of the people entering the world in that time will be born in countries where the problems of hunger are the worst.

A JOB FOR SCIENCE AND TECHNOLOGY?

Handicapped by limited land and water, dwindling topsoil, and environment-threatening food production methods, the challenge to feed the growing numbers of humans is formidable. In such crises, humans have come to rely on the inventiveness of science and technology for solutions.

Science can be defined as the systematic collection of knowledge through study and experimentation. It involves the formulation of hypotheses, or educated guesses, in an area of study and the collection of data to either prove or disprove the hypotheses. Guesses that cannot be supported by fact are discarded regardless of traditional thinking or emotional beliefs.

Technology is sometimes referred to as applied science. It is concerned with making use of knowledge to produce practical inventions that allow humans to do what they previously could not do. The two disciplines feed each other: technology making use of scientific knowledge to design new instruments, science making use of technological advances to undertake new experiments that uncover new knowledge.

Science and technology have provided humans with many tools to extract more food from the environment. At the same time these tools have created a new set of complex environmental and social problems. Science and technology are not magic wands that can fix any problem. Just as there are limits on the capacity of the earth to provide sustenance and to absorb abuse, there are limits to what scientific know-how and technological inventiveness can accomplish. There are also wise and foolish uses of science and technology. Science and technology do not make choices. They only serve those who do.

For millions of human beings, there is no room for error in the choices we make concerning world hunger. A wrong choice is a death sentence for unimaginable numbers of the weakest and most innocent of our fellow humans.

CHAPTER 2
HUNGER—WHAT IT IS AND WHAT CAUSES IT

MORE THAN AN EMPTY STOMACH

The reality of hunger in the world is almost too hideous to ponder. One of the most common ways to avoid facing unpleasant facts, like those about hunger, is to dilute the language. Thus, for some affluent people, "hunger" means that empty feeling in the stomach late in the morning. "Starving" means missing a meal altogether and feeling more than a little uncomfortable about it. "Malnutrition" means not eating enough of the foods that provide basic nutrients.

A more precise definition of these terms gives a more accurate view of what the issue is all about. The following are five terms commonly used when speaking about world hunger.[43]

1. "Hunger" can be defined as a group of symptoms that come about because of a shortage of food in the body. It involves far more than the discomfort of an empty stomach. Hunger slows down the body's activity and makes it weaker.

2. "Undernourishment" refers to a situation in which a person does not eat enough food to sustain normal life. Units of energy-producing food are usually expressed as calories. The United States government estimates that the average adult's energy requirements are 2,400 calories per day.[44]

3. "Malnourishment" means that the person lacks both the amount and the quality of food needed to support normal life. The human body does not run solely on the energy provided by calories. It requires at least forty-five essential nutrients from food.[45] A shortage of any of these can result in serious health problems. When statistics are cited to show that there are 700 million malnourished people in the world, it means that 700 million people are seriously at risk because they are not getting essential nutrients.

4. "Famine" is a hunger situation that strikes a geographical area. It is usually triggered by a disaster, either natural (drought) or man-made (war). A famine means that large numbers of people have lost all means of obtaining enough food to survive. The sheer magnitude of suffering in famine-stricken areas attracts far more attention than does the ordinary, day-to-day hunger that many people live with. Yet the quieter, almost invisible form of hunger kills far more people than do the terrible famines.

5. "Starvation" is an extreme form of malnourishment in which the body begins to devour its vital proteins in a desperate attempt to get the nutrients it needs.

WHAT HAPPENS IN STARVATION

As long as fresh supplies of energy and nutrients are fed into its system, the body either grows or sustains its current level. When more food comes in than is required for growth or maintenance, the body stores some of the surplus as fat. When less comes in than is required, growth or maintenance is no longer possible. Unable to shut off its systems completely without causing immediate death, the body turns to stored food to keep it going.

A normal, healthy person has enough fat stored up to keep the body functioning for several days. Since this fat is not used for any other purpose, it can be burned up with no ill effects on the body. Once these reserves of fat are gone, however, continued food deprivation becomes serious. The only available resource left is useful, functioning material, such as proteins in the muscles and organs.[46]

An adult human body can stand to lose about 30 percent of its weight, 10 percent of its water content, perhaps 30 percent of its minerals, and up to 15 percent of its proteins without suffering permanent damage.[47] Growing children are more vulnerable to the effects of hunger—they can tolerate much smaller losses before damage sets in. Once these levels are exceeded, starvation occurs. At that point, the body begins to devour vital tissues. Organs such as the liver and brain begin to break down until they cease to function. This is death by starvation.

While such a sequence illustrates the extreme brutality of hunger, it is only a small part of the devastation caused by inadequate diet. Even in the

earlier stages of malnutrition and starvation, the body grows steadily weaker. The body cannot keep warm; its defenses against disease break down. Infectious diseases such as tuberculosis, which has been greatly reduced in more affluent societies, kill many people weakened by hunger.

Deficiency diseases caused by malnutrition can strike down victims long before they starve to death. Deadly conditions such as beriberi, pellagra, and scurvy result from a shortage of certain vitamins.

Lack of proper protein in the diet is the most widespread nutritional problem of all.[48] The protein-deficiency disease kwashiorkor often develops in Third World children after their first year. Its most obvious symptom is a swelling of tissues that, ironically, may cause the child to appear healthy, if not overweight. But the death rate for kwashiorkor may be as high as 80 percent.

Even when the ravages of hunger do not end in death, they can easily prevent victims from living a normal life. Malnourished adults become listless and apathetic, irritable, and unable to concentrate. They fall into a brutal cycle, being unable to perform productive tasks that might help them acquire more food.[49] Malnourished children do not grow properly. Even if the malnutrition lasts only for a short while, the lost growth potential can never be

A young famine victim in Ethiopia. Growing children are particularly vulnerable to the effects of hunger.

regained. The most obvious evidence of this is in stunted physical growth. But just as common and far more tragic is the hidden devastation of stunted mental capacity.

The brain grows at a much faster rate than does the rest of the body.[50] At the age of a year-and-a-half, 80 percent of a human's eleven billion brain cells have already been formed. By the age of four, the child's brain has already achieved 90 percent of its adult weight while its body weight is closer to 20 percent.

The concentration of brain growth in the early years of life means that proper nutrition during those years is critical for mental development. A shortage of proteins in an infant's diet means the child will be unable to synthesize proteins to form brain cells at the normal rate. Once a child falls behind normal brain development, he cannot make it up. A short period of malnutrition results in below-average levels of intelligence. This retardation of brain development can occur even before birth. Malnutrition causes poorly developed placentas in pregnant mothers, which slows the development of their fetuses.

Hunger does not have to be severe in order to inhibit brain development. A child may suffer permanent loss of intelligence even while appearing to be adequately fed and to be developing normally. Just a slight shortage of nutrients over a long period of time can cause the same damage as short-term starvation. A frustrated Brazilian doctor who works with the very poor of his country has charged that malnutrition is creating a race of people with almost no intellectual capacity.[51] While it is difficult to estimate how many minds have been affected by inadequate food levels, it is almost certainly over a billion.

CAUSES OF HUNGER

The world's farmers are churning out far more food per person than they have in centuries past. Yet the twentieth century is tormented by far more devastating famines than ever recorded in past history. Why is there so much hunger and starvation in the modern world? What causes the horrendous famines in which masses of children waste away and die in misery?

Natural Disasters

Farmers' battles against the fickleness of nature are well documented in literature and history books. Even city dwellers commonly deflect disappointment over a rainy day by commenting that "the farmers need the rain." It is a natural assumption, then, that food shortages result from unfavorable weather. Dry weather causes crops to wither in the field. Wet weather results in flooding that causes crops to rot in standing water. In either case the community is left with no food to eat. The more severe the weather problem, the worse the famine.

This has certainly been the case throughout much of history. Even as late as the seventeenth century, Europe experienced food shortages whenever the weather failed. Below-average harvests occurred about once every three years, and abnormally bad weather produced famine about once a decade.[52]

Despite the best efforts of science and technology, farmers continue to depend heavily on favorable weather to produce good crops. Reports on famine conditions in Third World countries reinforce the logic that bad weather causes poor harvests, which cause hunger. Pictures of cracked, parched farmlands supporting almost no vegetation make it easy to imagine food shortage and starvation. Africa, the continent with the most severe hunger problems, is saddled with a far more variable pattern of rainfall than is found on other continents.[53] The worst famines in Africa in the 1980s have followed periods of widespread rainfall failure. Some particularly unfortunate areas have gone more than a year without a drop of rain.

Yet there are two compelling pieces of evidence showing that droughts and floods are not the primary causes of hunger and starvation. First, droughts and floods occur all over the world, not just in hunger-stricken areas such as Africa, Latin America, and Southeast Asia. The United States has been struck by severe droughts an average of about once every twenty years.[54] In 1988 it suffered through one of its hottest and driest summers on record. Yet even though thousands of fields were devastated, there was no famine in the United States. China suffered almost as badly from drought as did the United States in 1988, yet this heavily populated country experienced no famine.

Second, hundreds of millions of people in Third World nations go without adequate nutrition even when the weather is favorable and local crop harvests are bountiful.

Many hunger analysts believe that the weather has become a convenient scapegoat that masks the real causes of hunger. It is more accurate to say that natural disasters provide a dramatic push that, combined with other factors, turns malnourished populations into starving ones.

War

Far more devastating than any natural disaster is the human-created disaster of war. Warfare and famine have gone hand in hand for as long as history has been recorded. War kills able-bodied workers; consumes labor, supplies, and money; restricts travel; and destroys roads, bridges, harbors, ports, buildings, and vehicles. Even relatively affluent industrial societies cannot escape the widespread hunger that accompanies prolonged warfare. Following World War II, much of Europe required massive food donations from the United States to stave off starvation.

While any kind of war disrupts a nation's economy, civil war causes the greatest suffering. Not only does civil war involve physical destruction of property and human life, but it shatters the stability of a society. Civil war is waged by desperate, determined people who will often go to almost any length to aid their cause. This plunges the country into lawlessness and chaos.

Civil war has recently ravaged the countries of El Salvador, Nicaragua, Ethiopia, Mozambique, Angola, the Sudan, and Cambodia, to name a few. Those countries have experienced some of the worst famines in modern times.

In the Sudan in 1988, favorable rains produced the best harvest in a decade. Yet 4 million Sudanese faced starvation, thanks to a brutal conflict between the government and rebels in the south.[55] In the

Sudan's civil war, both sides have used food as a weapon. Government troops have imposed blockades on entire cities in the rebel-held south, hoping to starve out the rebels. One city went eight months without receiving any food shipments.

The rebels solved their problem by taking what little food the civilians had. Despite the mass starvation of innocent people, the government refused to cooperate with international relief efforts, fearing that the food would all end up in the hands of the rebels. There was no shortage of food in the Sudan, nor of relief workers, nor of transportation for the food. Yet the state of war caused the starvation deaths of thousands.

The situation was even worse during that same year in Mozambique,[56] where rebel forces conducted a campaign of terror to dislodge the government. More than a million people were driven from their homes by the cruelty of the rebels and the outlaws who flourished among the chaos caused by the rebels. Farmers were attacked and killed, their crops burned, and their property destroyed. Two million farmers stopped planting crops altogether, fearing that anything they grew would be ruined anyway.

This left more than 6 million of Mozambique's 15 million people in grave danger of starvation. Again, relief groups waited in the wings to supply food to the starving. But with rebel troops threatening to shoot down Red Cross planes, there was little that could be done.

Warfare further aggravates the problems of hunger by uprooting people from their homes. Millions of refugees have fled their communities in places such as Afghanistan, Somalia, and Cambodia to escape the battle zones and campaigns of terror. These refugees often bring nothing with them when they escape. They have no means of producing food, nor any money with which to buy it. Often they flood neighboring areas that are already strapped to feed their own people and cannot support the influx. The Sudan generously welcomed many Ethiopian refugees of the 1984 and 1985 famine. The hundreds of thousands of rootless, nonproductive people certainly contributed to the Sudan's own hunger problems a few years later.

Overpopulation

In the opening chapter we briefly discussed rapid acceleration of the world's population. The growing magnitude of the world hunger problem is often viewed as evidence that the limits of human population have already been reached.

There is no question that some Third World nations are placing far more demand on the land than it can supply. Again, Africa can be viewed as the prime example. Farmers are driven to produce more crops from the land and to expand into marginal grazing lands in order to meet increased demand. This quickly wears out the relatively thin soil in many parts of the continent. As the population increases, more and more land is driven into infertility. The result is an ever-increasing food shortage.

Again, however, hunger experts point out that severe hunger can be found in many underpopulated areas of Central Africa. Both Latin America and Africa, the two neediest regions, have a considerable amount of arable land that is not in use. At the same time, some of the world's most densely populated sections, parts of Southeast Asia, have been able to feed their people.

Hunger and starvation in our present world,

then, cannot be blamed on overpopulation. Again, it is more accurate to say that the addition of millions of people every day compounds the problem of feeding the world. It makes it difficult for many nations to keep food production ahead of food supply and presents grave problems for the future. Greater population densities also mean that a disaster of any kind will likely affect a greater number of people.

Overconsumption
Industrial nations consume far more of the world's resources than do Third World nations. If the critical factor in overpopulation is the amount of demand placed on the environment, then it is the industrial nations that are approaching the limits of what the earth can support.

This overconsumption carries over into the area of food supplies. From 1965 to 1975 Americans added 350 pounds of grain to their average yearly diet, most of it in the form of grain-fed meat.[57] This additional amount is about equal to the total food consumption of the average Indian in a year. Assuming that Americans were already well-nourished in 1965, this addition amounts to squandering the world's food supply.

Much of the increase in consumption is due to the insistence of affluent people that meat be a dominant part of their diets. Raising livestock for food is not necessarily a poor use of the earth's resources. Livestock can make use of pasture lands that are not suitable for supporting food crops. In an effort to boost profits, however, industrialized nations are increasingly abandoning grazing land. Instead, they raise livestock in concentrated feedlots, where the animals are fed corn from prime farmland instead of forage from marginal cropland. More than a quarter of the grain grown in the world winds up in the stomachs of livestock instead of humans.[58] These animals do not make very efficient use of the grain. It takes at least four pounds of grain to produce a pound of pork and at least eight pounds of grain to produce a pound of beef.[59]

The conversion of grain into alcohol is an even more glaring waste of the world's food supply. Billions of bushels of food staples, such as barley, potatoes, corn, rye, and rice, are converted each year into alcoholic beverages. Aside from the harmful effects of these beverages, they have virtually no nutritional food value.

Brazil has experimented with another form of food-to-alcohol conversion. During the 1970s, when the price of oil was skyrocketing, its government tried to find a cheaper, cleaner, alternative fuel. Their solution was to produce ethanol from sugar cane. In 1984 Brazil had 400 ethanol conversion plants in operation. While millions of acres of land were used to grow this cane, Brazil had to spend a billion dollars that year to buy grain from other countries.[60]

The above examples have been used to imply that livestock, alcoholic beverages, and ethanol are taking food out of the mouths of the world's hungry people. In a world where land, water, and other resources for growing food are limited, it may well be that humans cannot afford such inefficient use of the world's grain supply. But, again, stockpiles of grain have been accumulating even as much of the world starves. Therefore overconsumption of food by industrial nations cannot be seen as a significant cause of hunger currently rampant in the world.

The overconsumption of other resources by industrialized countries may hit closer to the real cause of hunger. The insatiable demand of industrialized countries for far more than their share of natural resources has led to fertilizer shortages and higher fuel prices. Both of these hinder the ability of Third World farmers to grow food. More importantly, they make it more difficult for poor people to earn a living. Hunger analysts insist that it is this inability to earn a living that is at the root of most hunger in the world today.

Poverty
Hunger is the most acute symptom of poverty—the inability to earn a living. Being too poor to lead a normal life means being too hungry to lead a normal life.

The reason why Americans eat well in times of drought while many Third World people starve during a drought is money. Wealthy people can bring food in from outside communities that have not been affected by drought. Poor people cannot. When food is scarce and expensive, the wealthy can afford to pay higher prices for it. Poor people cannot. Wealthy people can invest in machines, fertilizer, and special seeds to increase their yields. Poor people cannot. Wealthy people can afford to hold onto their land even in shaky financial times. Poor people cannot.

Bangladesh suffered through a terrible famine in 1943, despite the fact that their food supply was actually higher than the year before. The reason? Inflation had cut the purchasing power of the poor so badly that they could not afford to buy the food. India has commonly had warehouses filled with grain during times of famine because the poor cannot afford to buy it.[61]

Hunger and poverty are so closely connected that the statistics for the two are practically identical. It has been estimated that about 750 million of the world's people live in absolute poverty. In other words, they are unable to grow enough or earn enough to supply their basic needs. That corresponds very closely with the number of chronically hungry in the world. An estimated 2 billion people are seriously poor or destitute. This figure corresponds closely with combined estimates of the numbers of protein-deficient and stunted or hunger-damaged people.[62]

Poverty is also a primary cause of the population expansion that looms ahead. Large families are especially important to people who have no assets in life other than children, nothing to support them in their old age other than children. Poverty causes children to die, and so parents wanting a large family must have many children to ensure that enough will survive. Poverty also means that money and education are not available for those who wish to practice birth control.

Government Policies

Certainly government policies that lead to or perpetuate warfare are direct causes of serious hunger problems. But there have been other planned strategies that have contributed to poverty and hunger.

Many Third World nations have attempted to bridge the economic gap between them and the industrial nations by concentrating their efforts on urban industry. They have passed laws catering to the wants of urban dwellers.[63] For example, governments have often kept the price of food low. In so doing, they have ignored agriculture, which is the means of support for about 80 percent of Third World workers. Many of these farmers cannot survive on the prices they are being paid for their produce.

Government investment, educational opportunities, and welfare programs, too, are often concentrated in the urban communities at the expense of the rural areas. Farmers are forced to fend for themselves against increasingly long odds.

Those who believe firmly in free trade argue that socialistic meddling has created considerable poverty. It is pointed out that a number of the world's poorest countries have socialist governments. Socialist governments have been attractive to Third World countries because they have promised economic equality to poor people who have been severely oppressed. In fact, China appears to have achieved success in reducing hunger through socialist policies.[64] Other socialist governments, however, have ruined local economies by overzealous government planning. The forced relocation of villages and the formation of collective farms from private land has worsened the lot of many of the world's poor. Government control has stifled initiative and creativity and often has failed to reward those who work hard.

But while socialist planning has created its own ills for the world's poor, free-market enterprise has done the same. A number of people have made their fortunes by exploiting the starving. During a severe drought, a poor farmer with no means of feeding his family is often faced with an impossible choice. If he sells his land in order to get food, he will reduce his ability to support himself the next year. But if he does not sell the land, his children will starve to death.

Severe famine forces many poor to lose what little land they own. Since a starving family has no choice but to sell, this leaves them in a poor bargaining position. Their land can be snapped up at low prices by wealthy people who can afford to buy land even in hard times.

Further, the price of any product on the free market is governed by supply and demand. When the supply of food is abundant, the price goes down. When it is scarce, it is in high demand, and therefore people are willing to pay more for it. Therefore, during good harvests the farmer receives a low price for his food. When his crop fails, food is likely to be scarce all around. If he then has to buy food, he must pay top price. Either way, he loses.

Speculators have taken advantage of this to make fortunes during times of famine. When the weather is bad and famine starts to strike, they hoard grain. They know that the longer the famine goes on, the more valuable the grain is and the better price they can command for it. So, while others are dying of hunger, they sit on their stores of grain and wait for the price to go up. Some of the richest families in the Bengal state of India accumulated incredible fortunes in this way during the famine of 1943.[65]

The lure of a handsome profit has also provided an incentive for harmful ecological habits. It is far more profitable in the short run for a person to farm intensively and to dump fertilizer and pesticides on the land. The long-term destructive effects on the environment can be left for future generations to worry about.

International Policies
Third World nations are experiencing increasing problems competing on an international scale. Many of them are deeply in debt to Western nations. The prices they receive for their products have been going down, while the prices they pay for imports have gone up. The produce section of a typical United States supermarket demonstrates the disparity. Bananas grown thousands of miles away in Latin America or Central Africa cost the consumer a third as much per pound as apples from an orchard five miles out of town. During the past ten years, Africa has lost 20 percent of its purchasing power on the international market.[66]

Just as individuals who cannot support themselves fall into a cycle of misery and despair, the same happens to nations. Money that could be invested in equipment, supplies, and transportation facilities must instead be used to pay off massive debts.

It is here that the overconsumption of resources by the industrial world is called into question. Industrial nations use far more than their share of the world's natural resources to produce their wealth. By this irresponsible use of the earth's resources they increase their competitive advantage over poorer countries, driving them into greater poverty and therefore the greater likelihood of famine.

Another form of overconsumption is the enormous share of the world's resources that is spent on weapons.[67] The annual amount spent on developing and acquiring instruments and armies of destruction has climbed to over 500 billion dollars. The United States spends more money each year on weapons than the combined incomes of the world's poorest billion people. Fearful of aggressive neighbors who have armed themselves to the teeth, Third World nations have been forced to divert enormous sums of money desperately needed for constructive uses into the military budget.

Injustice

Injustice thrives wherever power is concentrated in the hands of a few, where large groups of people have no voice in their government's decisions. Injustice causes starvation in a number of ways.

1. Colonial Legacy. Part of the plight of Third World nations is a carryover from the days of European domination. European explorers and settlers claimed many of these countries as colonies and looked upon them as cheap sources of raw materials for both them and their countries. As masters of these new colonies, they often claimed the best land for themselves. Native peoples were pushed to lands that were unable to support large numbers of people. The nation of South Africa provides an apt illustration. South Africans of European descent own 80 percent of the land (which is also the best land) despite a population that is less than one-sixth that of native Africans.

Although the colonies have largely achieved political independence, the land inequity has seldom been corrected. Those who were moved off the land never got back on. The great bulk of Third World people are farmers who do not have enough land to provide for more than the most meager living. In

Africa, three-fourths of the people own approximately 4 percent of the land.[68] In Latin America, a third of the population lives on 1 percent of the cropland.

Those shunted onto poorer land have been pushed by necessity into destructive land-use practices. The rural poor of Brazil, locked out of the nation's prime farmlands, resort to clearing rain forests. They grow enough to survive until the soil wears out after a few years and is lost forever as productive land. Africa's deserts grow as poor herders try to raise their livestock on land too fragile to support them.

Colonial settlers also introduced the practice of growing cash crops in place of food crops. Cash crops are those specialty crops that are grown for export rather than for local consumption. Sugar, bananas, coffee, tea, cocoa, cotton, and rubber are some prime examples. Profit motives also prompt landowners to plant cash crops even in areas desperately needing food. Such crops command far higher prices from foreigners than landowners can hope to receive from locals for food crops.

Cash cropping creates a number of hunger-related problems. For one thing, it removes prime agricultural land from grain production. It takes food away from those who need it in order to produce goods for foreign people who are already well-fed. In Haiti, peasants were forced off the richest farmlands, which were then used to grow cocoa, coffee, and sugar for the wealthy.[69] Many nations have made millions of dollars on cash crop exports while they were unable to provide for the basic nutritional needs of their people. That is why Brazil became the second leading exporter of food in the

1980s at a time when more than 80 million of its people were dangerously underfed.[70]

Cash crops also exhaust the soil very quickly. Many acres of land that once easily supported a mixture of crops in Western Africa have been leached of their nutrients by cash crops.

2. Corrupt Leaders. A number of the world's poorest nations are run by individuals who line their own pockets at the expense of the poor. Haiti, home of one of the world's most destitute populations, has been bled dry by corruption. Among the most outrageous injustices inflicted by its former leader, Prosper Avril, was the $10,000 fee that was charged to any Haitian relief agency that received foreign aid.[71] Concern over government misuse of funds caused most of the international aid available to Haiti to be suspended or withdrawn during the Avril regime.

Some rulers have spent millions of dollars on weapons and other military equipment to prop up their regimes. Meanwhile, millions of their countrymen go hungry, and money for investment cannot be found.

3. Societal Traditions. In industrial countries as well as Third World countries, poverty is encouraged by traditional attitudes toward women.[72] Woman have been denied status, education, ownership of land, or meaningful employment. They have been forced to rely on men to provide the means for their existence. When there is no man to rely on, women are often left with no means of support. As a result, the vast majority of starving adults in the world are women.

Attitudes toward women also fuel the population explosion. In many societies, the only claim that a women has to status is her ability to bear many children. This creates intense interest in having as many children as possible.

Other groups have been purposely barred from the opportunity to improve their lives. India's caste system separates the very poor from the rest of society in a group known as "untouchables." South Africa's apartheid system to keep the races separate accomplishes the same thing. By restricting the rights of poor groups, the wealthy are able to keep the wealth for themselves.

The following chapter shows how all the above-mentioned factors can combine to weave a web of misery in the modern world.

CHAPTER 3
CASE STUDY IN HUNGER: ETHIOPIA

Hunger is often hidden in the quiet agonies of children in a lonely village, or in the dull, vacant stare of a malnourished family. If there is one place in the world where the horror of starvation has been laid out in the open for all to see, it has been Ethiopia.

The devastation in Ethiopia in the mid-1980s took many people by surprise. Yet virtually all the causes of hunger mentioned above are so plainly visible in that country that catastrophe was inevitable. Human choices paved every step of the way, as if the human race was determined to build a highway to hell. The agony of the Ethiopian people makes for a painful study. But an understanding of their situation is necessary if such famine is to be prevented in the future.

Ethiopia is approximately 1,200,000 square kilometers (463,000 sq. miles) in area, and is located on the Eastern Horn of Africa.[73] It is a land with an ancient history, much of which has included the specter of hunger. Drought and famine have been documented in Ethiopian records for more than 2,200 years.

Eritrean rebels in Ethiopia. Their long
struggle against the central government
led to a "quarantine" of their region, which
cut off desperately needed supplies. This
was but one of a series of factors that
contributed to widespread famine in the nation.

BLAME IT ON THE DROUGHT

On the surface, Ethiopia appears to be a prime example of the theory that the cruelty of nature is responsible for famine. Ethiopia contains one of the hottest deserts in the world and a good deal of dry, semi-barren highlands. Rainfall has never been reliable in that corner of the world. The normal "wet" season is from late June to September, but there have been many years in which little rain has fallen. Even when the rains come, they may fall so hard that they wash away nutrients in the soil.

Famine has been a regular visitor to Ethiopia. Since the sixteenth century, the country has suffered a serious food shortage an average of once every eleven years. In 1888, an estimated one-third of the population died of hunger-related causes. The 1983 dry season was just about on schedule. Eleven years after the last serious drought, the Ethiopian plains were again dust dry. This drought was especially severe. The woeful cycle of famine turned into a holocaust that killed hundreds of thousands outright and damaged millions of others.[74]

Closer inspection reveals, however, that it was far more than shortage of rain that caused the worst famine in the country's history. Ethiopia was a disaster waiting to happen.

FIRST INVITATION TO FAMINE: POVERTY

The great majority of its citizens were mired in poverty.[75] At the time of the famine, Ethiopia was estimated to have the lowest standard of living of all African nations. The average Ethiopian earned roughly $110 in a year. Despite sitting across a narrow gulf from oil-soaked Saudi Arabia, the country had few reserves of energy. Oil imports alone consumed more than a fifth of the country's export earnings in a year. What little wealth the country owned was concentrated in the hands of a few.

Many Ethiopians had too little food even in the best of times. Malaria, tuberculosis, and other diseases flourished among the hungry. Hospitals and other health facilities were almost nonexistent. As a result, the life expectancy for the average Ethiopian was about twenty-five years less than for those in industrialized nations.

The educational system was so poor that most of its citizens could not read or write, with estimates of illiteracy running from 60 to 90 percent. Ethiopia's internal transportation system was so threadbare that most of its citizens were isolated from the rest of the country. In 1980, Ethiopia had only one railroad line and had fewer roads per square mile than any other country in Africa. More than three-fourths of the farmers in Ethiopia had to walk a half-mile to reach the nearest all-weather road.

SECOND INVITATION TO FAMINE: RAPID POPULATION GROWTH

Ethiopia's population was estimated to be around 32 million in 1980. But with poor access to so much of the country, it was difficult to get an accurate count. Later reports showed that the government's official estimate had been short by nearly 9 million. Because of this error, the country's reckoning of its food available per person had been way off.[76]

Poverty-stricken Ethiopian families depended on children as their only assets and security in life. With so many of their children dying in the first year of life, these families needed to produce many children in order to ensure that enough of them survived. Thus Ethiopia's population was galloping ahead at better than 3 percent per year. That meant that within twenty-five years a country that was already struggling to feed its citizens would have twice as many people to feed.

THIRD INVITATION TO FAMINE: ECOLOGICAL DESTRUCTION

More than four out of five Ethiopians lived in rural areas, where they supported themselves by raising crops or tending livestock. The land on which they lived was often marginally suited to the task. Much of the best land was reserved for growing cash crops instead of food for the local population. Coffee was Ethiopia's most profitable export.

Forests that had once covered most of the land were cleared away for agriculture. But the thin soils could not support the European method of intensive farming. Winds came up and, unbroken by tree cover, swept the land of its precious nutrients. The sparse grasslands could not support the growing livestock population, which was thought to be the largest in Africa. Overgrazing and overfarming turned large tracts of moderately productive land into barren ground.

FOURTH INVITATION TO FAMINE: WAR

It was Ethiopia's tragic misfortune to then be locked into not one, not two, but many bitter wars at the same time. Many Africans do not feel any loyalty to arbitrary boundaries drawn up by central governments in which they have little say. The people of the far northern province of Eritrea have been battling the government of Ethiopia ever since they were annexed in 1952.

In 1974 a separate revolution toppled the monarchy of Emperor Haile Selassie. In Selassie's place, a military Marxist government was installed. The authority of this new government was never recognized by the people of Eritrea. The neighboring province of Tigre began its own fight for independence in 1977. Altogether, more than twenty different groups within Ethiopia have been battling the government in the past decade.[77] As if this were not more than any country could stand, in 1980 Ethiopia became engaged in a war with its eastern neighbor Somalia over disputed territory. The effects of war have been as devastating as always. Hundreds of thousands of people fled their homes in areas of conflict. In order to purchase weapons for waging war, the government sold needed grain to the Soviet Union. The government sealed off desperately needed wells and water holes to prevent their enemies from making use of them. The government was also reluctant to allow aid in for their enemies in the northern provinces.[78]

FIFTH INVITATION TO FAMINE: DESTRUCTIVE GOVERNMENT POLICIES

The government attempted to overhaul Ethiopia's economy and turn it into a pure socialist state. The callous and destructive way in which this was carried out merely multiplied the country's woes. The way of life that the villages had developed over the centuries was wrecked. More than 600,000 Ethiopians were uprooted from the north and moved to the more fertile south. Left without support, more than 100,000 of these transplants died.[79]

The government demanded that all crops be sold to the state for whatever price the government chose to pay. The official price was set so low that farmers could not afford to grow the crops. Precious farmland lay empty even while the drought tightened its grip over the country. Some farmers who did work the land were paid so little that they could not afford to pay their taxes. They were taken to prison, and their land and animals were confiscated. Under this system, even the Wollaita district in the south, normally productive even in dry weather, could not grow enough to support the population.[80]

Unwilling to provide any evidence that it was failing to provide for the basic needs of its people, the government played down and even denied the existence of starvation. Many people in the Ethiopian capital of Addis Ababa remained unaware of conditions a hundred miles away.[81] Not until the famine had raged for a year did the outside world begin to understand its magnitude. Led by the tireless efforts of people such as rock singer Bob Geldof, the industrial nations responded with billions of dollars' worth of food, equipment, and personnel.

By the time help came, however, the worst of the damage had already been done. Millions had already been uprooted from their land and now had no way of earning a living. Government bungling added to the suffering even when relief was pouring in. In order to control every facet of the economy, the state set up a huge bureaucracy that choked the system with red tape. Relief workers were hassled about travel permits, fuel permits, and driver's licenses. Supplies from foreign countries were left sitting on docks for weeks while forms were processed. Dying children who did not have the proper papers were turned away from hospitals.[82]

SIXTH INVITATION TO FAMINE: INJUSTICE

The most galling contribution to Ethiopia's plight was the indifference and corruption of its leaders. Ethiopia's ruler, Mengistu Haile Mariam, and his aides paraded around in expensive automobiles and other trappings of pomp. During the peak of the famine, while thousands of his countrymen wallowed in misery, Mengistu spent an estimated 100 million dollars throwing a lavish party to celebrate the tenth anniversary of his coming to power.[83]

All these factors were like tinder-dry prairie waiting for a spark to set off a wildfire. The drought provided the flame. In 1984 the country became a land of unspeakable horror.[84] Gray, shriveled figures, covered with flies, lay in the streets, in ditches, or in crowded camps. Some cried, some stared in a glassy stupor, waiting to die. Some villages were abandoned, others littered with people too weak to leave in search of food. Children carried their tiny brothers and sisters for miles to refugee camps and make-shift hospitals. They came, not in the hope of finding relief for their siblings, but simply to know how long they had to live.

Crowded camps and fouled water brought on dysentery, typhoid, hepatitis, and cholera. Malnutrition brought with it kwashiorkor and tuberculosis. Many died shivering in the early hours of morning, with no flesh on them to keep them warm. In the morning, men with shovels went out to prepare the graves, so that those left without dignity in life might have at least the dignity of burial.

The smallest children were sacrificed first, their food given to the stronger ones. It was a brutal matter of survival. For it was the adults who had to survive if any of the family were to live through the famine.

Eventually more than a billion dollars in aid reached Ethiopia. Development groups helped dig wells and build roads and bridges. They planted millions of trees and demonstrated farming methods, such as terracing, that would prevent land erosion. The rains were good during the growing seasons of 1984 and 1985.

But famine continued to haunt Ethiopia. When rains again failed in the summer of 1987, starvation returned in full force. The basic conditions had not changed; in fact, they had grown worse. The population had continued to grow. The land showed little promise that it could deliver more food, and so the country faced an annual shortage of two million tons of food.

Many of the people had used up the last of their resources in the great famine—their land, their animals, their property. Their chances of earning a living were worse than ever. Nearly a million refugees had fled their drought-stricken homelands. What chance did these uprooted, landless people have of producing their own food? Warfare had grown ever more grim and savage. Whereas all sides had refrained from attacking relief groups in 1984–1985, that restraint appeared to have run its course. Food convoys and distribution centers were ravaged. By the end of 1989, more than 100 relief vehicles had been blown up and hundreds of tons of food destroyed by raiders.[85]

There is not yet an end in sight to the tragedy of hunger in Ethiopia.

CHAPTER 4

THE LONG FIGHT AGAINST HUNGER

Although we do not yet know the maximum number of people that can be supported by the earth, we do know that limits exist. The earth's capacity to support life is determined by the amount of energy available from the sun and the amount of resources available from the earth.

Human populations have increased dramatically over the past 10,000 years. Yet neither available solar energy nor the earth's resources have increased noticeably during that time. What has changed is the proportion of the earth's life-supporting capacity that has been used to support human life, and much of this change is due to science and technology.

Earlier human societies existed by gathering wild food and hunting wild animals. These food sources made up a very tiny portion of the living things supported by the earth. As long as humans were forced to rely on these relatively scarce food supplies, their populations remained relatively small. Estimates of the maximum stable population of the earth during this period have been set at about 8 million persons.[86] When unfavorable weather reduced the growth of those plants and animals needed by humans, or when humans grew too numerous to be supported by the food supply, people starved.

Humans, however, learned to alter their habitats to suit their needs. At around 8000 B.C., societies developed ways to make the earth produce more of the plants that they could eat, at the expense of those plants they could not eat. This was accomplished by clearing existing plants off the soil and replacing them entirely with desirable food plants. Historians have called this drastic change the "Agricultural Revolution."

Farming produced far more food for humans than did hunting and gathering, and so human populations grew substantially. This did not by any means eliminate hunger in the world, though. Just as before, unfavorable weather could wipe out the food source, and societies could outgrow the ability of the land to consistently provide enough food.

Hunger was again the result. However, now the increased numbers of people meant starvation on a far broader scale than during hunting and gathering times.[87] The Egyptians recorded the first historical evidence of widespread famine in 3500 B.C. Famine has been a regular affliction of human populations ever since. The Roman Empire suffered from repeated, sustained periods of starvation. Chinese records show at least 1,800 separate instances of famine in various provinces over the past 2,000 years. Great Britain has identified more than 200 famines during its past 1,000 years of history.

In recent times, as the earth's population has swelled ever higher, famines have taken an ever more horrendous toll on human life. France lost millions of people, possibly one-third of its population, to starvation in the early eighteenth century. Another period of famine in that country eighty years later triggered the French Revolution.

During that same century, failure of the potato crop in Ireland slashed that country's population in half, from 8 million to 4 million. At least one-tenth of the population, and probably much more, died of starvation in Bengal, India, in the 1800s, and an estimated 9 to 13 million Chinese died of hunger-related causes in China from 1876 to 1879.[88]

In the nineteenth century, the ravages of the Bolshevik Revolution brought on a famine that killed millions of Russians. Millions more Europeans died of hunger during and following World War II. While written records in Africa and South America have been sketchy, recent repeated outbreaks of starvation on those continents have shown that those areas have seen more than their share of hunger-induced misery.[89]

In response to the greater magnitude of starvation in the twentieth century, numerous private organizations have been formed to combat world hunger. The efforts began with the work of the Red Cross and the American Friends Service Committee (AFCS) following the two world wars. The growing family of such relief efforts was joined by CARE, Oxfam, and the United Nations Children's Fund (UNICEF) in the 1940s and World Vision in the 1950s. Since then more groups have organized, including The Hunger Project, Bread for the World, Live Aid rock concert fund-raising, and many more, including a wide spectrum of church groups.

TRADITIONAL PROTECTORS
AGAINST HUNGER

Plants

The vast majority of the world's people depend on plants for their major source of nutrition. Although there are more than 350,000 known species of plants on the earth, humans have cultivated only about 150 for food purposes.[90] Of these plants, by far the most significant have been the cereal grains: rice, wheat, and corn. These cereals provide over half of the calories consumed by the human race.

Many more people depend on rice for survival than on any other living thing.[91] It is the principle crop of Central and Southeast Asia, where population densities are the greatest. Rice has some limitations as a food staple because it contains a small percentage of needed protein. But it can thrive in a wide variety of climates and is especially suited to the water-soaked farmlands of Southeast Asia.

More of the earth's farmland is devoted to wheat than to any other crop.[92] Higher in protein content than rice, it satisfies about 20 percent of the calorie requirements and nearly 45 percent of the protein requirements of the world. Since its water requirements are relatively meager, it can be grown on vast plains that receive little rain. Ninety percent of the croplands in the Northern Hemisphere are devoted to wheat.

Corn, or maize, is the staple food of more than 200 million people.[93] Although its protein content is below that of wheat and its water requirements are higher, its extremely high yields per acre make it a popular crop. The United States produces more corn than any other crop. Most of it is used, however, as livestock feed.

Oats, rye, sorghum, and millet are less common cereal grains that, nevertheless, also provide basic nutrition for millions of people.

Legumes, such as soybeans and chickpeas, are important crops because of their protein content, which can be three times that of wheat. Potatoes, while lower in protein percentage than the cereals, produce five times as much food per acre as the cereal grains. A relative of the potato, the cassava, has been called the "poorest man's staff of life." Despite containing only 1 percent protein, the high-yield cassava is mainly responsible for keeping 500 million South Americans, Africans, and Asians alive.[94]

Animals

Animal products (meat and dairy) provide about 17 percent of the world's calories.[95] Their use is associated with affluent countries because of the inefficiency of animals as a food source. It takes approximately 2 pounds of grain feed to produce a pound of chicken meat, 4 pounds to produce a pound of pork, and more than 8 pounds to produce a pound of beef.

The three cereal grains, rice (top left), wheat (top right), and corn (below), together provide over half of the calories consumed by the human race.

Animals, however, can make use of the nutrition in grasslands that are too dry to economically produce food crops. Nearly two-thirds of the land used for agriculture is devoted to animal forage.[96] Also, about one-fourth of the animal protein consumed by the world comes from the sea.

THE GREEN REVOLUTION

The late 1950s and early 1960s were a time of complacency about the world's food situation. Following the hardships of World War II, world economic conditions improved steadily. Upon leaving office in 1960, United States President Eisenhower declared that the world had gone through its first famine-free decade. With scientific progress on all fronts, including such high-profile areas as space exploration, it seemed likely that humans could easily solve the basic problem of providing food.

The introduction of vaccines, antibiotics, pesticides, and other health technology, however, fueled a tremendous spurt in population growth rates of Third World countries. A large percentage of the increased food production was consumed by population growth. All it took to explode the myth of a world of plenty was a two-year drought in Asia during 1966 and 1967. Suddenly a billion people were facing severe food shortages, far worse than at any other time in the world's history. Population forecasters such as Paul Ehrlich predicted that the runaway growth of population was far exceeding the limits of the environment and that some of the poorest countries were in such impossible straits as to be beyond help.[97]

At the same time, the Western countries began to

take a serious look at the damage their high-production societies were doing to the environment. Evidence indicated that increased production might compound the environmental problems plaguing modern man. If humans could not safely increase production, what hope was there of feeding these billions of babies coming into the world? A horrendous famine seemed likely.

Near the end of that great drought, however, the Green Revolution came to the rescue. Actually, this movement had its roots in 1943 when a privately funded research center began looking into ways to improve crop yields.[98] The rationale was simple. If a plant could be made to double the amount of usable food it made, than the world food supply would double without any further taxing of the environment.

The most widely heralded of these researchers was Dr. Norman Borlaug. Working in Mexico, Borlaug developed dwarf wheat varieties that put less of their energy into plant structure and more into usable food. Beginning in 1967, the new seeds developed by researchers became widely available. Not only were there high-yield varieties, but also drought-resistant strains for use in arid lands.

The benefits of this new generation of improved seeds were dramatic. During the late 1960s, grain production increased by 5 to 6 percent, about double the rate of population growth. Third World countries with a history of famine problems showed a marked improvement in yields. Some fields produced three times as much grain per acre as in previous years. Wheat production in India doubled in just four years.[99]

The success of the miracle seeds was so sudden

Dr. Norman Borlaug, who developed dwarf,
high-yield varieties of wheat.
For his contributions to the so-called
Green Revolution, Dr. Borlaug was
awarded the Nobel Peace Prize in 1970.

and dramatic that a new era in agriculture was proclaimed—the Green Revolution. It was considered by many to be the most significant agricultural advancement since the Agricultural Revolution. Norman Borlaug's contribution to the world food supply was considered so significant that he was awarded the Nobel Peace Prize in 1970.

The Green Revolution continued to sweep through the croplands during the 1970s. The United States' corn output in 1975 was double that of 1960.[100] India, which the pessimists of the 1960s had declared to be beyond hope, actually produced enough grain to support itself. By the early to mid-1980s, Green Revolution seeds were used in half the world's rice and wheat fields, providing more than 50 million extra tons of grain. World grain production climbed from 631 million metric tons in 1950 to 1.65 billion metric tons in 1984. Mexico was growing nearly four times more wheat in 1983 than it had in 1965.[101]

But while some proclaimed victory in the battle against hunger, others were more skeptical. For one thing, the drastic growth in yields was not entirely due to the new seeds. The early plantings of these seeds were blessed with favorable weather, a situation that inflated the impact of the Green Revolution. Researchers then determined that much of the increase was due to added amounts of fertilizer prescribed for the growing of these high-yield crops. That 250 percent increase in grain production had been obtained with a 900 percent increase in fertilizer use.[102]

It was also pointed out that those wonderful production figures could not have been possible without a 300 percent increase in irrigation or an increase in the amount of marginal land brought into cultivation.

Green Revolution farming also opened up a whole new set of problems in the battle against world hunger. This new method of farming required far greater use of fuel and modern farming equipment than was being used by most small farmers. Poor farmers who tried to take advantage of the Green Revolution were unable to raise the money to buy the seeds, let alone the fertilizer, the pesticides, or the equipment. As a result, only wealthy farmers benefited from the new seeds. Their increased output caused a glut of grain that drove the market price of wheat lower. Unable to afford the price of the new technology, the poor could not increase their production to make up for the lower price. The Green Revolution put them farther behind than they were when it started.

By the mid-1980s, it had become apparent that the Green Revolution had not been a revolution at all. Although the rate of population growth was slowing, food production in many parts of the world could not keep up with it. Even though the world was feeding a billion more people by the end of the 1980s than it had in 1970, there were more hungry people in the world than ever before. During the 1970s, some 80 million Africans suffered from chronic hunger and malnutrition. In the 1980s that number climbed past 100 million.[103] At best, the wondrous technology of the Green Revolution had only bought time for the world to come up with a better answer to the persistent problem of hunger. In many countries the main result of the Green Revolution has been to increase the gap between the rich and the poor.

CHAPTER 5
IMPROVING BASIC
FOOD TECHNOLOGY

MECHANIZATION

The transition in farming from human labor to mechanized labor has entirely changed not only the face of farming but of Western society as a whole. Little more than a century ago the United States, for example, was primarily a rural society. Large numbers of farmers working on their small farms produced enough food to support an average of five people per farmer. By the 1970s, the average farmer was feeding sixty-five.[104] That left great numbers of people free to perform other jobs.

There are two main purposes in bringing machines into agriculture: to cut down on the amount of physical labor that the farmer has to do and to make the process of farming more efficient. In terms of overall production, making the farmer's job less strenuous is not as important as an improvement in efficiency. The mechanized products of modern technology can till more land, plant more seed, apply more fertilizer, and harvest more crops in a

Productivity of the average U.S. farmer
has increased over thirty fold in the
last one hundred years. Mechanization
has been a key factor.

given length of time than a person can do without them. This increased efficiency means that an individual farmer can produce far more food than was possible in the days before machines. During the early 1900s, a farmer needed to work an average of about 100 hours in order to produce 100 bushels of corn. Now it takes fewer than twenty hours of labor to grow the same amount.[105]

Agricultural machines have been improved over the years to accomplish an increasing number of tasks with greater efficiency. Harvester-thresher combines, for example, can collect the grain off vast tracts of ripe fields in a short period of time, while leaving behind less than 3 percent of the product. It is possible that further improvements in design and engineering will produce machines that can accomplish more tasks with even greater efficiency.

Mechanized farming has not been an unqualified blessing, however. Despite its emphasis on efficiency, modern, mechanized farming is efficient only in terms of the amount of manual labor saved. It is not efficient in terms of energy use. In a mechanized system, farmers use an average of eighty gallons of gasoline to grow a single acre of corn.[106] Such high consumption is increasingly serious in times of energy shortages and concerns over atmospheric carbon.

Mechanized farming is also enormously expensive. Even a modest stable of machinery costs hundreds of thousands of dollars. Also, the more complex the machinery, the more training or education is needed to operate it properly. Both of these facts put an enormous burden on the farmer.

In industrial countries, the emphasis on expensive machinery and high technology puts the small farmer at a disadvantage against huge industrial farms that have the money and knowledge to exploit the latest technology. In the areas most desperate for food, the effect is even more disturbing. For the average Third World farmer, even the most basic machines are often too expensive and the technology too foreign to consider. Only wealthier farmers are able to make use of the equipment. This greatly increases their efficiency and adds to their profits. The already yawning gap between rich and poor grows wider. Poor farmers, less able to compete, are forced off the land and left without any means of making a living. Unless they are made affordable and training can be provided, mechanical means of farming will not increase production for the bulk of the world's farmers.

While mechanized farming can produce more food in less time and with less effort than manual labor, it cannot do anything about increasing the total amount of food that the land can produce. The primary effect of mechanization, then, is to reduce the number of farmers. In areas of the world where there is a surplus of humans looking for meaningful work, this is hardly a blessing.

Mechanized farming has also increased the problem of monoculture crops described earlier. While humans are able to perform a wide variety of tasks, a piece of machinery can perform only a limited number of them. The advantage of a machine is that it can perform a great number of repetitions at great speed. In order to make use of machines, agriculture has had to reduce the number of tasks required, while increasing the number of repetitions of that task.

Lawn mowers illustrate this principle. A riding

lawn mower is able to cut more grass at a time than a walk-behind mower. The walking mower is more versatile. In a yard filled with trees, shrubs, a sand box, and a swing set, the riding mower's increased mechanization is useless. The diversity of the terrain restricts its cutting ability. On an open field with no obstructions, however, the only task is high-speed repetition of a single function. Here a riding mower can make use of its superior cutting ability.

In order to make best use of farm machinery, farmers plant large fields with a single crop in which all the seeds are planted the same way, and all are harvested the same way. As discussed before, a single, homogenous plant community makes poor use of the available nutrients and can be easily devastated by a single insect or disease.

The introduction of machinery and the mono-crop systems that accompany its use into Third World countries often cause more damage than good.[107] Any future use of mechanical technology to boost food production must be appropriate for the farmers who use it. Technology must cease to give advantages to the rich and must be aimed at the limited resources of the small farmer.

FERTILIZERS

Over the past half-century, the most important weapon in the fight against hunger has been chemical fertilizers. It is estimated that at least a third of the increase in food production over this time has been accomplished by using manufactured fertilizers.[108] While improved strains of grain received most the credit for the Green Revolution of the

1960s and 1970s, at least half the increase in Third World crop yields in those two decades came about because of increased fertilizer use. At this moment, approximately one-and-a-half billion people are living on food that would not exist without the use of fertilizers.

Fertilizers are simply concentrated doses of the chemical elements that plants must have in order to grow. Of the twenty such required elements the most important are nitrogen, phosphorus, and potassium.[109]

Fertile soil contains enough of these chemicals to meet the needs of many plants. Since different plants use different amounts of these elements, the soil can support a complex plant community without being depleted of any one element.

The balance, however, is considerably altered by the monocrop fields required by mechanized agriculture. Grain crops are particularly heavy users of nitrogen. Nitrogen is necessary for the formation of amino acids, which are the building blocks of proteins. Few soils contain enough nitrogen to sustain a wheat field for very long. The thriving plants suck the nitrogen out of the soil, and when the wheat is harvested the nitrogen is removed from the system. The only way to keep nitrogen in a wheat field is to periodically add high-nitrogen fertilizer to the soil.

Fertilizers are not a cure-all for future food shortages, however. They cannot indefinitely add to the ability of the land to produce the crops we desire. They are already being used to their peak effectiveness in many fields and are of little use in areas where water is the primary limiting factor.

The cost of producing chemical fertilizers is high, and that cost must, initially, be paid by the farmer. For the 80 percent of the world's poor who live as subsistence farmers, chemical fertilizers are yet another luxury they cannot afford.

Fertilizer production also requires the use of nonrenewable resources, not only to power the processing equipment but to provide the raw materials for fertilizer. Natural gas, for example, is used to make ammonia, a form of nitrogen often used in fertilizer. The world does not contain an endless supply of natural gas, which is also heavily used for heating homes.

There are other environmental concerns connected with chemical fertilizers. Not all of the chemicals are transferred to the soil and to the plants. Fertilizer run-off can seep into groundwater drinking supplies and collect in rivers and lakes, feeding the growth of algae that choke the life out of water systems. Fertilizer factories produce further pollution.

Because of these problems, agronomists are focusing on two alternate means of fertilization. One of them, the use of organic fertilizer, is a return to traditional methods of agriculture. Manure from animals is rich in chemicals and nutrients and is a far cheaper source of these materials than is chemical fertilizer. It is basically a recycling system that keeps the natural community in balance.

One disadvantage of this, however, is that concentrated organic material can pollute groundwater, rivers, and lakes as effectively as can chemicals. Further, in many poorer areas of the world, manure is needed to supply energy for fires.

The second alternative involves research with nitrogen-fixing bacteria. Nitrogen is one of the most abundant elements in the world—it is the most abundant element in the air that we breathe. Unfortunately, many plants, especially cereal crops, lack the ability to make use of nitrogen from the air. However, some bacteria can convert atmospheric nitrogen into a form usable by plants. Rhizobium bacteria live in the roots of plants known as legumes, a group that includes soybeans, alfalfa, and peanuts. Because of the action of these bacteria, plants can collect nitrogen without taking it from the soil.

Nitrogen-fixing plants could reduce the demand for artificial nitrogen fertilizers in two ways. First, more of them could be used as food crops. Second, nitrogen-fixing plants could be periodically grown and plowed back into cropland, thus restoring nitrogen to the soil.

WEED AND PEST CONTROL

Humans are not the only species fighting a battle against hunger. Since the earth's resources are limited, we are constantly at war with all other living things over the use of those resources.

Modern agriculture has provided the battleground for some of the most intense turf wars ever fought. Our efforts to make the land produce more food for humans have also made life easier for those life forms that share our taste in food. Vast tracts of fertile soil, tilled and fertilized, are ripe environments for whatever seeds can establish their roots the fastest. Thick rows of grain laid out neatly for harvesting convenience also act as overflowing tables of food laid out for whatever else can get there first.

Weeds, insects, fungi, bacteria, viruses, and worms all compete with us for the fruits of our agriculture. About a third of all crops in the field are lost to these rivals. The most bountiful crop in the United States, corn, is under attack from thirty different pests and fifty different diseases. Potatoes are prime targets of more than 260 known invaders.[110]

At least 2,000 species of weeds create problems for farmers by crowding out and reducing the growth of desirable plants.[111] Many of these plants can germinate more quickly than food crops and can survive under harsher conditions. Wild oats alone have been blamed for more than a billion dollars' worth of crop loss in a single year. Giant foxtail and redroot pigweed can rob a cornfield of as much as a quarter of its grain potential. Noxious weeds in pasturelands cause the death of up to 5 percent of the United States' livestock.[112]

More than 8,000 species of insects feast on crops in the United States alone.[113] When given an abundant food source, insects can multiply at an incredible rate. Great clouds of grasshoppers have been known to strip a field bare in seconds. The corn borer, the potato leaf hopper, the velvet bean caterpillar, and the Mediterranean fruit fly are a small sampling of the most destructive of these creatures.

Plant parasites in the form of bacteria, fungi, worms, and viruses can be the most destructive of all usurpers of human crops. Entire fields and flocks can be wiped out by one of these plagues. Bacteria are particularly harmful to fruits and vegetables. But microbes also cause some of the blights, wilts, and leaf spots that attack plants such as alfalfa, wheat, and corn. Many chickens are killed every year by a bacterial-induced disease known as coccidiosis.

Root rot, rusts, and smuts caused by fungal in-

The corn borer is but one of the multitude
of pests that afflict crops in the
United States. Crops under extensive cultivation
are particularly susceptible to such blights.

fection damage a wide variety of plants. Mosaics and dwarfing are some of the destructive results of viral damage. Small roundworms known as nematodes collect their share of the farm product, consuming 7 percent of all United States crops.[114]

Until the early middle of the twentieth century, humans had few methods of protecting crops against the encroachment of all these competitors. At that time, chemists began assembling an array of chemical poisons to do the job. One of the most effective of these weapons was DDT. Originally synthesized in 1874, DDT was developed for pesticide use in the 1940s. Since then, the market has been flooded with products designed to kill specific crop enemies. Pesticide use in the United States has mushroomed from zero in the early 1940s to more than 5 billion pounds per year in the late 1980s.[115]

Yet, by all accounts, the war against our tiny competitors is not going well. There are certainly cases in which pesticides have prevented runaway destruction. But in the long run, the use of pesticides appears to be likely to cause more harm to ourselves than to pests. Agricultural experts have pointed out that despite this massive dumping of poisons into the environment we have made little, if any, progress in reducing crop losses from weeds, disease, and insects![116]

The main reason for this is the ability of these small, rapidly reproducing organisms to develop resistance to poisons. Some insect species that were once controlled by DDT have developed strains that can tolerate high doses of the chemical. Bacteria can mutate even more quickly than can insects into new, toxin-tolerant forms. The net result of the pesticide war has been that more and more poison is needed to achieve the same results. In many cases only a tiny percentage of this shower of poison actually reaches the pests. Pesticides have been known to do more damage than good by killing off insects and birds that eat some of the more harmful crop destroyers.

While the pests are developing immunities to these chemicals, the poisons are accumulating in our environment. Some of them, including DDT, linger in a toxic state for many years. Already this accumulation has reached levels that are dangerous to humans in localized areas.

With the mounting health concerns about chemical pesticides, scientific research has increasingly turned to biological warfare. Biological pest control is hardly a new notion. For centuries, people have used cats to control rodent populations. The use of biological controls in agriculture, however, has been largely neglected in favor of the quick chemical fix.

One of the first instances of the use of biological warfare was in the early twentieth century when selected beetles and moths were used to control the spread of the prickly pear cactus in India and Australia.[117] In the United States in the early twentieth century, the California orange crop was attacked by tiny lice that fed on the sap of the trees. Researchers discovered that the pest was native to Australia, where it was naturally controlled by a species of ladybird. The ladybird was brought to California, and it soon brought the lice under control.

Currently, research is under way to discover more natural predators of harmful organisms. Microbiologists are looking at bacteria, protozoa, and viruses that attack specific crop destroyers without harming the rest of the environment.

Another biological tool is sterilization. This has proven effective in battling such pests as the screwworm. By sterilizing male screwworms and releasing them into screwworm breeding grounds, scientists have been able to prevent the rapid reproduction of the cattle nemesis.

STORAGE AND PROCESSING

The world's food supply is not safe even after it is picked from the fields. Another 30 percent of food products is lost during storage and processing.[118]

Rats in North America and birds in Africa steal billions of dollars' worth of food stored for human consumption. The construction of better barriers between food and animals and the observance of more sanitary procedures could stop some of these losses.

Food loss from spoilage is an even greater problem. The decomposition of plant and animal material, performed by bacteria, is a necessary step in the recycling of materials in nature. But it also means that much of the food we grow remains in an edible state for only a short time before it begins to rot. The perishable nature of food has been a severe limitation on the world's food supply since humans first appeared on the earth.

Early attempts to keep food fresh included drying and salting, methods that are still in use today. Smoking and pickling are two more techniques developed to inhibit the growth of bacteria.

Sealing food from contact with air is another basic strategy. Originally pottery and glass jars were used for this purpose. It was not until the nineteenth century that the first tin can factory was introduced in London. After slow initial acceptance, canned food began to grow in popularity in the early twentieth century.[119]

Extremely low and high temperatures are now two of the most common means of food preservation. Ice chests have long been used, where ice was available, to take advantage of the fact that a cold temperature retards the decaying process. Mechanical devices to create cold temperatures were developed in the 1910s. Within a few decades, refrigerators and freezers were in wide use in industrialized countries.

Ever since Louis Pasteur proved the role of bacteria in food spoilage in the nineteenth century, heat has been used to kill bacteria in food. Milk and many canned goods are subjected to heat processing.

The twentieth century has brought other innovate techniques of food preservation. Drying techniques were improved during the 1930s and 1940s, followed by vaccuum packing and freeze-drying. The most recent food-preservation technology makes use of radiation. A brief burst of radiation can keep strawberries fresh for thirty days and meat good for six months.[120] Radiation technology, if consumer fears about safety and health hazards can be overcome, could offer considerable improvement in food preservation.

The primary problem with modern food-processing techniques is their inefficient use of energy. In 1910 the entire food production chain—from seed to plate—consumed slightly less energy than was produced by the food. By 1970, the food system was using up nine times as much energy as it produced.[121] Processing often uses up more energy than is required to grow the food. Further, modern food processing relies heavily on disposable materials such as steel and plastic. This has created an enormous solid waste disposal problem that will continue to get worse as landfills take up more and more space on the planet. Two crucial challenges for science and technology are to find ways of cutting down on energy use in food processing and to develop a better system of recycling materials.

DISTRIBUTION

Currently, enough food is produced to provide every person on earth with 3,600 calories per day.[122] This is well above the 2,400 needed for a healthy diet. At the same time, there is widespread hunger.

The contrast is particularly frustrating in those countries that have a large number of starving people. Brazil has become the world's second largest food exporter, yet more than 80 million Brazilians are in desperate need of food.[123] In South Africa, thousands of children die from inadequate diets every year while the country ships food to other nations. During one of Bangladesh's worst famines, in 1974, there actually was enough food in the country for everyone to have survived. Obviously, it does not matter how much food we produce if we cannot distribute that food to the people who need it.

The uneven distribution of food across the earth is hardly a new problem. Throughout history, most famines have been local in nature. When the rains failed in a particular area, the shortage of food affected everyone in that area. It made no difference that harvests were lush several hundred miles away because it was difficult to get food from one place to another.

The severity of local droughts and food shortages has been softened by improved methods of transportation. Science and technology have developed trains, trucks, ocean ships, and airplanes that can quickly move food supplies from overstocked lands to desperately needy people.

A quick walk through a grocery store in any industrial nation demonstrates the effectiveness of modern transportation systems in distributing food. In the United States, shoppers at any supermarket can buy bananas from Africa; coffee, fruit, and beef from South America; fish from New Zealand and Alaska; beer from Germany; and imported specialties from Europe and Asia. United States and Canadian farmers have been supplying wheat to many parts of the world.

Obviously, science and technology have already developed adequate means for distributing food. This technology needs to be made available to Third World nations where many farmers must walk miles to reach the nearest road.

The greater problem in distribution is not a matter of technology. With the physical means of distributing food now widely available, it is primarily economic and political barriers that prevent food from getting where it needs to go.

IRRIGATION

Proper use of irrigation has been used to more than double yields in lands limited by dry climate. As described earlier, however, a limited amount of water is available for irrigation. In addition, many of the side effects of irrigation have also proven disastrous. One of the worst problems is the accumulation of salts. As water is spread out into hot, dry lands, fast evaporation leaves a concentration of salt on the land. Few plants can grow in areas that build up too high a salt content.

The drying of the Aral Sea, described earlier, has left salt wastelands. These salts are blown into the air, sometimes creating salt storms that travel hundreds of miles. Salt dust can present serious health hazards, especially to the human respiratory system. Irrigation projects in Africa's Sahel region have faced similar problems, with the hot, dry climate evaporating most of the water before it can be used.

Irrigation has also been blamed for spawning diseases. Standing irrigation water in Egypt, for example, has led to outbreaks of a parasitic disease known as schistosomiasis.[124]

Scientific solutions proposed for the water shortage include ambitious projects such as the use of seawater. So far, the problem of salt removal has proven too costly and inefficient to allow for this water to be used for crops. An even more ambitious scheme would be the towing of icebergs, which contain huge amounts of fresh water, to areas where water is needed. While such solutions have been presented, little evidence suggests that such projects will be carried out in the near future.

Presently, irrigation technology is focusing on more efficient use of water. This means lining irrigation canals with concrete or plastic to prevent water seepage into ground where it is not needed and constructing underground irrigation canals to prevent evaporative loss. Methods of recycling irrigation water are also being researched.

BREEDING

By far the greatest impact of science and technology on world food production in recent years has been in the area of genetics, or breeding. Plant and animal breeding has been carried out on an informal basis for centuries. It has long been noticed that offspring of animals tend to take after their parents. Animals that displayed desired qualities were favored for their ability to produce offspring with similar characteristics.

Similarly, plant breeding consisted mainly of the favoring of varieties that exhibited desirable traits. Wine producers, in particular, have been very selective over the centuries about what varieties of grapes to grow.

The systematic study of breeding did not really begin, however, until the work of an Austrian monk named Gregor Mendel during the 1860s. Mendel's experiments with plants demonstrated that plants passed on characteristics to future generations in predictable ways. The scientific study of the transfer of characteristics from one generation to the next became known as genetics.

The study of genetics demonstrated how cross-breeding between two individuals with different characteristics could produce a combination of those characteristics in the offspring. The trick for researchers was to find ways to pass on desirable traits to offspring without passing on undesirable ones.

Scientific experiments were able to produce a number of new varieties of plants in which desired characteristics from two different varieties were combined. These plants, known as hybrids, were introduced to farmers during the 1930s. Hybrid plants often grew faster, showed greater resistance to drought or diseases, and produced higher yields than purebred plants. Their use is credited with a large increase in food production during the period from the 1930s to the 1950s.[125]

During the 1950s, researchers were able to cross-breed wheat and rye to form a new grain called triticale. This new plant combined the flavor and nutritional value of wheat with the hardier nature of rye. The combination enabled farmers to grow a wheatlike crop in harsh, dry areas that would not support regular wheat.

The Green Revolution was heralded as proof of what could be accomplished with plant selection and breeding. The high-yield wheat varieties developed by Norman Borlaug provided tons of additional food for the world without using any additional land.

Plant genetics offers some promising avenues for increasing the world's food supply. One goal of researchers is to produce varieties of food, particularly cereal grains, with greater nutritional value. Agronomists could concentrate on breeding, for example, strains of rice that put a greater percentage of their energy into protein production and less into carbohydrate production. This could increase the protein supply for a majority of the world's people without requiring the use of any additional resources.

The need for pesticides could be curtailed if varieties of grain with natural resistance to insects and disease could be developed. Wild plants often undergo their own natural breeding through the process of natural selection. Those plants that develop natural control against predators gain an advantage over those that do not. Therefore, wild plants in their native habitats frequently have inherited strong resistance to pests. By crossing highly productive domestic plants with the wild forms, high resistance can be bred into crops. This was successfully accomplished with varieties of corn during the 1970s.[126]

More than 150 million acres in Asia would be well suited to agriculture if it were not for the toxic salt content of the land.[127] Researchers are seeking a way to make use of this land by breeding plants with greater tolerance for salt. Brazilian researchers have announced the development of a type of corn that can thrive in the toxic, aluminum-rich soil of the Cerrado plateau.[128] Even contaminated lands could be made productive by crops that were bred to thrive on pollution.

Researchers have long been interested in developing plants that grow deeper roots as a means of obtaining water during periods of drought. The Japanese, meanwhile, have been aiming in the other direction. With much of Eastern Asia flooded by rains each year, the Japanese have been attempting to find forms of wheat and soy that can grow well in water-soaked fields.[129] These high-protein crops would greatly increase the protein supply in that part of the world.

There have been proposals to develop crops with a high tolerance for herbicides. Farmers growing such crops could then douse their fields with greater amounts of the poison. By so doing they could greatly reduce the weed population without the need for any mechanical weeding. There are, however, grave environmental concerns associated with any plan that calls for increasing the amount of poison dumped on our fields.

Agronomists have also been attempting to increase yields by strengthening the tendency of some plants to grow and mature quickly and of others to produce well under crowded conditions. The benefits that can be gained from developing a single, improved strain of cereal are so high that seed companies, universities, and governments pour millions of dollars into seed research and development programs.

Animal breeders, too, can work on producing fast-growing, disease-resistant livestock. Genetic methods of selecting for animals that are more efficient at converting plant material into usable protein might be used. One experiment along this line has been the "beefalo"—a cross between a cow and a bison. This is an attempt to combine the bison's ability to grow on less nutritious rangeland with the cow's more flavorful meat.

While plant and animal breeding has proven to be a relatively clean method of increasing food production, however, it has caused a potentially serious problem of its own. The hazards of monocrop farming, mentioned earlier, are magnified by genetic uniformity.

It is only natural that a farmer will want to plant the best seed available. When plant breeders develop a type of wheat with qualities that are superior to other wheat, therefore, most farmers are going to plant that type of wheat. Other types of wheat will fall into disuse and gradually disappear. The same holds true for breeds of animals. This heavy reliance on a single variety of a single species puts us in a vulnerable position for two reasons. First, a single disease or insect could wipe out a huge portion of the world's wheat at once. This is especially true of new hybrid plants that have taken the place of native species, which have had many years of genetic adjusting to their habitats.

Second, the loss of variety leaves scientists with a shrinking "gene pool." This means that there are fewer varieties of plants to draw on for future breeding work. Plant breeders are working to preserve and expand the gene pool by collecting and storing many varieties of commercially important plants, including wild forms of the plants. These varieties are stored in seed banks for future use.

CHAPTER 6
FOOD TECHNOLOGY
OF THE FUTURE

GENETIC ENGINEERING

Plant and animal breeding has traditionally been accomplished by mating or cross-pollinating pairs of organisms. Recent explorations into the basic building blocks of life have uncovered a new tool for creating desirable life-forms. Scientists are now able to "program" desirable traits into the reproductive matter of a living cell. So instead of spending years in tedious experiments that combine all the genetic material of two organisms, scientists can isolate specific traits and either eliminate them or build them into the organism. Identical organisms can be obtained by "cloning" the original organism straight from its cellular material.

Genetic engineering, as this activity is called, can be traced to the discovery of DNA in 1953. The British team of Frances Crick and James Watson was the first to discover the structure of deoxyribonucleic acid (DNA), the basic chemical building block of living organisms. DNA consists of two spiraling strands of amino acids linked together like zippers. There are four amino acids involved in forming DNA strands, and these acids always occur in pairs.

All of the instructions for forming the proteins of an organism are contained in pieces of DNA known as genes. The sequence in which the four amino acids occur in this DNA determines the characteristics of the living matter to be formed.

A single-celled bacterium contains 9,000 genes, so it takes a great deal of research to determine which genes control which characteristics.[130] Once that is accomplished, a scientist can identify the sequence of amino acids that are the blueprint for the particular trait. That trait can then be changed simply by altering the sequence of amino acids in the gene.

In the 1970s scientists learned how to cut DNA strands to eliminate instructions for a certain trait and to splice in a different sequence of amino acids to produce instructions for a different trait. Gene-splicing, as this technique is called, offers a tremendous shortcut in the alteration and improvement of plant varieties. The goals of plant and animal breeding could be accomplished far more quickly with genetic engineering than with conventional breeding. For example, a researcher attempting to improve disease resistance in wheat could isolate a gene of resistance in a hardier plant. This gene can then be inserted into the DNA of the wheat. Any alterations in the wheat's DNA would be automatically passed on to future generations in the wheat's seed.

Genetic engineering could do more than simply speed up plant and animal improvement. For example, frost damage to crops in the field has been estimated to cost the food industry 14 billion dollars a year.[131] It was recently discovered that there are two kinds of bacteria, commonly found on plant leaves, that aid in the formation of frost. These bacteria contain a protein that is an ideal nucleus for the formation of ice crystals. Genetic engineering enabled a researcher to discover the genetic codes that caused the organisms to formulate this protein. He then created a mutated form of the bacteria by eliminating the code for protein formation. When the bacteria was released into a plant community, succeeding generations of the bacteria lost the frost-forming mechanism. As a result, plants were able to withstand temperatures as low as 23 degrees Fahrenheit ($-5°$ C) without frost damage.[132]

In June of 1980, the United States Supreme Court ruled by a narrow margin that genetically altered microbes could be patented. This opened the possibility of enormous profits from the formation of new human-engineered life forms. Currently private companies are making enormous investments in the area of genetic engineering.

During the 1970s microbiologists also became adept at cloning genes by reproducing exactly the original sequence of amino acids. This enabled scientists to produce an entire community of desirable organisms from a single exceptional parent. As an example, during the 1970s an English company cloned the very best oil palm plants it could find. Thousands of identical plants were produced from a single high-yielding plant. The result was a new generation of oil palms that produced 30 percent more oil than before.[133]

Cloning could have a profound impact on agriculture. Any individual plant that shows exceptional qualities of growth, yield, or resistance can be cloned so that an entire field of plants has those qualities. Experiments in which cotton plants were grown from plant tissue open the possibility that in the future clones of the most productive plants could be grown in a laboratory. A method of "factory farming" could be developed which would not require the use of soil at all. This would ease the burden placed on agricultural land. The disadvantage of doing this is that culturing plant tissues is an expensive process that requires a high input of nutrients.

NONCONVENTIONAL FOOD SOURCES

In some ways, the hungry people of the world are like a sailor floating on the ocean without any drinking water. The sailor is surrounded by water but he goes thirsty because none of it is in a form that his body can use. Similarly, the earth is brimming with plant and animal food. Unfortunately, so little of it is in a form that humans can use. Hundreds of thousands of species of plants, animals, and even bacteria, all storehouses of nutrition, go untouched.

One of the goals of biotechnology is to discover ways that humans can tap into these abundant, unused sources of energy.[134] Leaves, for example, are one of the most readily available sources of protein. Many forms of insects and animals derive their nutritional needs from leaves, yet humans do not. Experiments are under way to develop a means of concentrating the protein in leaves so that it can be used by humans.

The ocean has no shortage of fish, only a limited supply of those fish whose flavor is considered acceptable to humans. Inedible fish could be ground up and the valuable proteins isolated into a fish protein concentrate.

Insects reproduce at a prodigious rate, and many of them contain a higher percentage of usable protein than sirloin steak. Some insects, particularly grasshoppers and ants, are fried and eaten in some African and Latin American countries. Perhaps a way could be found to make insect protein palatable for more people.

Single-cell organisms may offer a less repulsive nutritional source. The concept of growing single-cell organisms for food is actually an ancient idea. Centuries ago, the Aztecs of Mexico harvested a blue-green algae from nearby waters.[135] Only recently, however, have researchers discovered what an excellent idea that was. Blue-green algae has been found to produce ten times the nutrition per acre as ordinary crops. Food producers have dabbled with the use of seaweed and algae from the ocean in high-nutrition food products.

Experiments with single-cell organisms have opened the possibility of indoor food production. In 1956 Japanese scientists isolated microbes capable of producing amino acids, the building blocks of proteins.[136] Since microbes reproduce in a matter of hours, compared to the many months required by livestock, they have enormous potential as a protein source. By growing them indoors, the unstable factor of weather in food production could be eliminated. Problems with soil erosion and overuse would also be minimized.

A combined venture of British and Italian researchers pioneered the way in single-cell protein production in the 1960s and 1970s.[137] They cultured various algae and bacteria (as well as multi-cell fungi) in large vats, using a residue of crude oil as an inexpensive food source. The microorganisms were then harvested from the vats, and a high-protein product was extracted from their dry cells. One form of bacteria was able to convert a methanol feedstock into a product with 70 percent protein content. Unfortunately, the oil shortages of the mid-1970s raised the price of oil too high for its use as a food source for microorganisms to be practical. Since then, research has continued using non-petroleum sources as a feedstock.

Another group of single-celled organisms known as yeasts has shown great promise at converting molasses into protein. Products of this process are currently used for animal feed but could be refined for human diets.

Multi-celled fungi have also been grown in vats supplied with plant starch or syrup and ammonia salts to produce nutritious mycoprotein. If such practices became widespread, they would convert surplus, low-protein crops into more valuable food sources. The most desirable material to feed these tiny organisms would be lignin-cellulose. This abundant structural component of plants is unusable as a food by humans, but is so common that it would be a cheap feedstock.

The use of any nonconventional food source is limited by consumer acceptance. Taste barriers could possibly be overcome by increasing sophistication in the chemical production of flavors and aromas. Texture, color, and appearance could be altered to suit consumers. Even so, the introduction of insects, fungi, yeast, seaweed, and rough fish to the diet would require a drastic change in attitude. In addition, batch-culturing of any kind presently demands a large amount of energy, both in the construction of facilities and in the operation of the fermentation vats.

OTHER BIOTECHNOLOGY

Biotechnology is being explored in other ways for means of increasing food production.

Hydroponics, the farming of plants in a water environment, is one possibility. If provided with the proper nutrients, hydroponic farms could make use of the water supply from lakes and ponds without the need for either soil or irrigation. Techniques could be developed for making plants more efficient in photosynthesis—the conversion of sunlight to organic energy. Vaccines could be developed to protect crops from the ravages of microbial diseases. A process could be developed by which more plants would be able to make use of atmospheric nitrogen and so eliminate the dependence on fertilizer. Microbiologists could discover which molecules regulate biological activity in plants. These molecules could be isolated, reproduced, and used to increase plant growth.

Biotechnical exploration is not limited to plant life. During the past decades, the use of artificial insemination has boosted livestock production. Sperm from high-quality males is collected and used to impregnate a great number of females. The process produces much the same results as plant cloning, in that one highly productive parent can be used to create thousands of offspring with similar genetic information. Researchers have carried this process a step further with frozen embryo transfers.

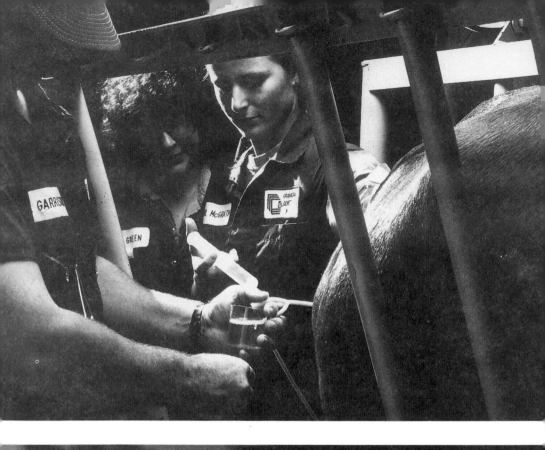

By this method, embryos from the union of two high-quality stock can be implanted in any female of the same species.

Metabolic steroids, the scourge of the sports world, have proven effective in increasing muscle content. Similar drugs could be used to increase the size and meat content of livestock. Future advances in livestock research could result in meat tissue and milk-producing glands being grown in laboratory vats, in a similar process to single-cell protein production. Drugs could be developed that cause animals to produce leaner meats.

The field of biotechnology is so new that its limits are unknown. Some hold out hope that super-crops and superlivestock can be developed in a short period of time. Perhaps a whole new realm of great-tasting, fast-growing, desert-thriving, pest-resistant crops can be produced. Why not a new breed of animal that can rapidly convert low-energy grasslands into delicious, protein-rich meat?

Top: Employees of
Granada BioSciences,
a Texas biotechnology
company, perform embryo
transfer in cattle.
Bottom: Granada cloned these
Holstein triplets in vitro
from a single embryo.
The clones were
transplanted to three
different mothers, who brought
the calves to term.

Such optimism, however, is tempered by the advice of Dr. Borlaug.[138] He points out that scientific research, for all its innovations, has never created an important new grain of any significance. "Do not look for a genetic solution to our problem," warns the father of the Green Revolution. Despite the extraordinary discoveries of genetics, there is currently no scientific breakthrough that offers an immediate promise of solving world hunger. Moreover, genetic engineering research is dominated by companies in the industrialized nations who are motivated by profit. Since the 1970s more than 600 biotechnology companies have been organized, most of them in the United States. The improvements they make are certain to go to those who can afford to pay for them. As a result, wealthy nations and wealthy farmers will again prosper, and the vast majority of the world's poor farmers will find themselves at a further disadvantage in competing for a share of the world market.

There are also reasons to fear the side effects of biotechnology, particularly genetic engineering. Natural communities have proven to be enormously complex. A bewildering array of organisms are interwoven in a vast web of interdependence in ways that we cannot fathom. Sometimes the removal or addition of one organism can entirely upset the balance of the community. Rabbits and toads overran Australia after they were introduced into the country by humans. Countless United States main streets stand shadeless because the Japanese beetle was accidentally brought into the country, where it has caused the destruction of elm trees. Much of the Southeastern United States has been overrun by a plant called kudzu, which was only recently introduced. Native Americans died by the thousands when exposed to unfamiliar forms of bacteria carried across the seas by New World explorers.

Anytime that humans tamper with the natural world the possibility exists for devastating damage. It has been a familiar pattern that technology brings along unwanted guests in its pursuit of higher standards of living. Technology has produced toxic wastes, the greenhouse effect, and the atomic bomb. What would happen if some untested bacterial mutant were to escape from a laboratory? Suppose a new plant being studied for its rapid growth were to get into the wild and begin crowding out important, slower-growing plants?

Biotechnology advocates stress that the risks can be determined beforehand. They believe that opponents are hurting progress by exaggerating the dangers involved. Ecologists, meanwhile, caution that even when great care is taken by researchers to evaluate all the possible effects of a new organism, natural ecosystems are so complex that it is not always possible to foresee all the possible consequences. Any decision to introduce a new seed or organism into the natural world is irreversible.

One solution to this dilemma might be the development of biodegradable mutants. These organisms could produce a great short-term benefit and then die out.[139]

CASE STUDY IN NEW FOOD TECHNOLOGY: BOVINE SOMATOTROPIN

Anxiety about rushing into technologies that we do not fully understand severely hampers the progress of biotechnology. The first major agricultural product to come from biotechnology has been bogged down in controversy from the moment it was unveiled. The stormy reception that greeted bovine somatotropin illustrates the problems that techniques such as genetic engineering must overcome if they are to make a significant contribution to the world food supply.

Bovine somatotropin (BST) is a natural protein produced by the pituitary gland of the cow. Also known as bovine growth hormone, or BGH, it is a long-chain molecule consisting of 191 amino acids.[140] BST is of great interest to the dairy industry because it stimulates milk and meat production in cows.

Researchers have used gene splicing to mass produce BST. The gene that programs BST production in the cow has been isolated and spliced into the genetic material of fast-growing bacteria. These bacteria are grown under controlled conditions in large fermentation vats, and the BST they produce is then collected.

In many ways, BST appears to be exactly the kind of product that genetic engineering is striving to produce. Preliminary estimates show that regular injections with BST will increase a cow's milk production by 10 to 25 percent.[141] Although the process requires some added protein in the cow's diet to make it work, the net result is that the BST-treated cows become more efficient at converting plant material into milk.

BST treatments are relatively simple, requiring nothing more than an injection of the hormone every two weeks or so. The cost is not expected to be outlandish, somewhere between twenty-five and fifty cents per day for each cow.[142] That amount will quickly be earned back in milk production. Further, the Medical Society of Wisconsin has reported that "bovine growth hormone produces no known unsafe biological, hormonal, or hazardous effects on humans, either directly or indirectly."[143] In fact, BST is already present in all cows' milk.

What more could agriculture ask than for a safe, natural substance that increases production by making better use of available resources? Manufacturers of BST proclaimed that it was ushering in a wonderful new era of farm productivity. The possibilities of growth hormone treatments seemed endless. They could increase meat production as well as milk production with the same grain-conversion efficiency. Porcine growth hormones could do the same for pigs. Better yet, it could reduce carcass fat in pigs by more than half and could increase the number of pigs per litter.

BST technology also has the advantage of strong economic backing from powerful sources. With the world market for BST estimated at between 500 million and 1 billion dollars per year, corporate interest is keen.[144] Several large corporations are currently producing BST; one of them has committed itself to a new 20-million-dollar facility for manufacturing the product.

Despite all the factors in its favor, however, BST has been shaken by withering fire from critics. Neither dairy farmers nor consumer groups have been willing to accept this biotechnology gift at face value. The European Parliament recommended prohibiting the sale of milk or meat from BST-treated cows. Several California dairy cooperatives refused to accept BST-treated milk. A group called the Foundation on Economic Trends requested that the

United States Food and Drug Administration perform an environmental impact study on BST before considering it for approval. In Wisconsin, the United States' leading dairy state, debate raged in the legislature over a bill to require labeling of milk from cows injected with BST.

The primary complaint has been that use of BST will upset the economic balance of dairy farming. United States dairy farmers have already been having trouble finding markets for their milk. In 1986 a million dairy cows were slaughtered under a government program to help reduce the milk glut in the United States. Opponents of BST fear that widespread use of the substance will create another glut that will drive down prices and force small dairy farmers out of business.

Some are afraid that widespread use of BST would follow the familiar pattern of lining the wealthy farmers' pockets at the expense of poorer farmers. In order to achieve the best results with BST, the cows' nutritional requirements will have to be met very precisely. Some experts believe that this will lead to the adoption of feeding stations where computers determine and ration out the nutrients for each cow. Computerized feeding stations would be expensive and could be used only by large-scale, agribusiness farms. Again, the small farmer would lose out.[145]

Finally, lingering doubts exist about tampering with the natural process. Some evidence indicates that BST may have an adverse effect on a cow's ability to reproduce. Farmers are also concerned about consumer acceptance of BST-produced milk. They fear that artificial shortcuts in the dairy process will destroy the wholesome, natural image of milk products.

As of 1990, the debate over bovine growth hormone showed no signs of fading away. When such controversy surrounds an effective, relatively simple, bioengineered product that poses no apparent hazards to human health or the environment, it does not bode well for the future of more exotic biotechnical techniques. It becomes apparent that biotechnology faces a difficult struggle in any efforts to create a breakthrough that will significantly expand the world's food supply.

VALUES

Science and technology have supplied solutions to a great number of world problems. However, science and technology are only tools that can be used by a society to achieve its goals. They do not determine what the goals of society should be.

The direction that a society takes to deal with major social problems can only be determined by the values that the society holds. A society built on greed and rugged individualism will be far less motivated to solve hunger concerns than one founded on charity and compassion. A society that values self-interest spends less effort on stopping hunger than one that values self-sacrifice.

Beyond that, philosophers have described two value systems that influence a society's moral understanding of its problems: formalism and utilitarianism. Formalism is the practice of strictly following basic, unchanging principles that apply equally to all situations. Formalists believe that these principles are the foundation upon which civilization is built, and so they are not to be tampered with even in exceptional cases. Utilitarianism, on the other hand, holds that the rightness of any action depends on the circumstances surrounding it. The test of morality for the utilitarian is whether or not the action benefits the greatest number of people in that situation.

Hunger concerns are not thought of as particularly controversial social issues. No one is in favor of hunger. Everyone agrees that it would be wonderful if every person had enough to eat.

There is, however, one major source of conflict between formalism and utilitarianism about hunger issues. That is the question of whether or not humans ought to provide assistance to those countries that are unable to feed their people.

DO NOTHING

One argument for a hands-off policy is based on the principle that hunger is nature's way of maintaining a balanced ecosystem. All life-forms, including humans, are competing for the limited resources of the earth. In a balanced ecosystem, factors such as predation, reproductive rates, disease, and longevity keep the competing populations fairly stable. A drastic change in any of these factors will upset the balance, and the population will either shrink or grow unchecked.

Unchecked population growth will eventually outstrip available resources. When that occurs, the excess population finds itself without the resources to support all its members. The unsupported members die of starvation, reducing the population to a number that can be sustained by the environment.

In this way, nature keeps the supply and demand in balance.

In the case of humans, stabilizing factors such as disease and longevity have been radically changed. This has allowed human populations to grow unchecked. No population can grow indefinitely on limited resources. When all else fails, nature will bring the population back into balance by means of starvation.

According to one utilitarian view, the sooner we can bring the population back into balance with the available resources, the better off we will be. Better to let nature take its course and let a few million starve now rather than let the population grow to several billion more than the earth can support.[146]

Massive aid efforts, such as those aimed at Ethiopia, India, and Bangladesh, have been criticized as harmful in the long run. Such aid does nothing to solve the long-term problem of hunger. It merely keeps people alive so that even more of them will be around to starve in the next famine. Relief efforts, it is argued, actually cause more suffering than they cure. They dump tons of grain into a poor economy, causing the price of grain to drop. The farmer who was producing just enough to survive may get so little for his crops that he is driven off his land and into starvation by efforts aimed at providing aid.

Further, foreign relief efforts can do little except reinforce the system that is already in place. The causes of hunger remain. The poor will still be poor, whether they are kept alive another year or not. Wars continue to rage regardless of what relief groups do. In some areas of the world, corruption is so rampant that there is little chance that aid will reach those for whom it is intended. By sending shipments to such places, relief groups are simply adding to the wealth of the dishonest.

There is also little point in sending aid to countries whose leaders do not take seriously their own responsibility to feed their people. In effect, aid sent to such places helps keep cruel, incompetent, or hostile governments in power. It solves, free of charge, a domestic crisis for them and leaves them free to spend money on arms or secret police. As a practical matter, if we offer any aid to a foreign power, it should be only to those governments we support.

Formalists would answer that it is easy for well-fed people to sit back and argue theories about long-term benefits. But what if you were the person who needed the aid? Ask the person whose life is saved or whose family is saved by emergency aid whether the relief was a good idea or not.

The formalist view is that every human being has the right to the basic necessities of life. It is repulsive to even think of forcing a small child to suffer the agony of death by starvation on the chance that it might make things better in the future. It is especially repugnant when there is currently more than enough grain in the world to feed everyone.

Formalists argue that humans are morally obligated to respond to the suffering of those in the present, while working to solve the problems of the future. The Green Revolution may not have solved the hunger problem, but it kept people alive.[147] Humanitarian aid and technological advances may not solve the hunger problem for the future, either. But they could eliminate suffering and keep people alive long enough for humans to come to grips with the real problems of hunger.

Many insist that there are more humanitarian solutions to the population problem than "letting nature take its course." Contraceptive devices, birth control education, economic incentives to decrease the birth rate, and even the more controversial method of abortion are more compassionate ways to hold the population to a supportable level than starvation.

Relief organizations also deny the charge that the grain they bring into a starving country brings down the price that local farmers receive for their grain. They argue that a farmer's market consists only of those people who are able to buy grain. Since the imported grain is given only to those who cannot pay for grain, it does not affect the farmer's market at all.[148]

Further, relief organizations recognize that temporary relief is not a solution to world hunger; it is an action to be taken in conjunction with other actions. Relief organizations are committed to using whatever resources they can to eliminate the causes of hunger. Many provide technical assistance and long-range development aid designed to help local communities make better use of their resources. They provide help in constructing schools, hospitals, wells, roads, and other means of improving life. Just because they do not have a magic cure for hunger does not mean they should pack up and go home.[149]

Humanitarian groups further argue that it is both cruel and foolish to allow innocent people to starve because of the corruption or incompetence of officials. More careful supervision and accounting procedures could reduce many of these problems. Many steps can be taken against governments or individuals that are particularly arrogant, unco-operative, or dishonest in dealing with foreign aid. Governments and charitable organizations can publicize these despicable actions and bring international pressure against those who conduct and encourage them.

The idea of providing aid only to those countries whose governments we support is totally inconsistent with formalism. It amounts to using food as a weapon to achieve political goals. If it is true that all human beings have a right to basic survival, then it is immoral to withhold those basics from them for any reason. It is outright barbaric to allow innocent children to starve to achieve political goals.

INCREASE PRODUCTION WITH MODERNIZED AGRICULTURE

The traditional approach to eliminating world hunger has been to increase the amount of food we grow. Those with a great deal of confidence in science and technology believe that human inventiveness will keep increasing crop yields as the need arises. History is on their side. Despite the rapid growth of the human population over the past centuries, the world food supply has more than kept pace.

United States farmers using modern machinery are producing many times more food than they produced a century ago. Most of the world's farmers are still using methods of agriculture that were used in the United States then. Once they are brought up to date, with tractors instead of oxen and combines instead of scythes, it stands to reason that they could greatly multiply their yields. Respected scientists have calculated that humans have the potential to grow enough food to support forty billion people—eight times the number living today.[150]

Others argue that modernization of agriculture has not achieved as much as it gets credit for. Prior to the early twentieth century, increased food production was accomplished primarily by plowing and seeding more land. That option appears to have just about closed. Most of the available farmland in the world is already being farmed, and some that is being farmed now is being lost.

Following World War II, food production soared because more food was grown on the same amount of land. Yields increased 400 percent within a couple of decades in countries such as India and Mexico. The United States' farms boosted their average yield by 175 percent from 1958 to 1981.[151]

But, as we have discussed, it is not the use of mechanized equipment that produced these increased yields. Fertilizer, irrigation, and hybrid seeds were responsible for most of the gains. Irrigation appears to have a limited role in providing further food increases. Fertilizer is expensive, is made from finite resources, and can reduce the productivity of the soil. Improved plant varieties appear to provide the most hope for the future. They have already sparked one Green Revolution, when genetic engineering was in its infancy. With modern methods of custom designing plants, it should be possible to create a great many useful varieties. Exotic technologies should be able to produce alternative food sources.

On the other hand, few improvements have been unqualified successes. They almost always involve trade-offs. Green Revolution seeds could provide

At a soilless rice seedling nursery in China,
workers roll up seedlings for transplantation.

greater yields but require more water and fertilizer. Researchers have developed a higher-protein wheat, but the benefit is canceled by lower yields. The reverse is also true: higher yielding wheat tends to have a lower protein content. High-yielding plants drain nutrients from the soil more quickly than lower-yielding varieties. Plants can be engineered to manufacture their own nitrogen fertilizer, but at the expense of plant growth. Single-celled protein can be grown in vats, but the energy required to process it into edible food is enormous.

Modern technology has been known to cause more harm than good in agriculture. Traditional methods of farming that have respected the delicate balance of the environment have been uprooted, with disastrous effects on the land. Thin African soils and Latin American rain forests have been destroyed by attempts to install modern, high-productivity farming. Industrialized monocrop farming with superstrains of plants creates easy prey for pests and diseases. Chemical poisons used in industrial farming endanger the environment while producing little long-term benefit for farmers.

The drive for greater production has caused a number of social problems as well. High-technology farming has favored the rich over the poor, increasing the inequity that results in hunger. It has created high unemployment and shattered ancient traditions and customs that have held communities together.

Finally, if the goal of agriculture is to make more efficient use of the earth's resources for human consumption, industrial agriculture has been going backwards. Such food production and processing techniques consume ten times as much energy as they produce.

SUSTAINABLE PRODUCTIVITY

The problem with high-productivity industrial farming, according to its critics, is that it is short-sighted. It feeds the present population by robbing resources from the future.

A permanent solution to concerns about the world's food supply cannot be reached until humans are in balance with the environment that supports them. This not only means that the population must be stabilized, but that our methods of producing food must be in harmony with nature. Science and technology should be used to develop ways of operating within this limitation.

Methods of increasing production that do not require great amounts of fossil energy must be developed. One way to do this would be to plant more efficient, nutritious crops. Soybeans, potatoes, and cassava are three examples.[152] Soybeans fix their own nitrogen, contain three times the protein of most grains, thrive in various climates, and are easy to harvest. More widespread farming of soybeans would greatly increase the world's protein supply. The potato and its warm-weather cousin, the cassava, require little cultivation, yet manufacture a huge amount of edible material per plant. Potatoes produce more calories and protein per acre of land than any other crop.

High-technology innovations must concentrate on helping plants and animals more efficiently convert raw materials into products that humans can use. Bovine growth hormone may be one such technology. These technologies should, however, be thoroughly tested for safety and be designed to benefit the poor at least as much as the rich.

The world's food supply will never be secure as

long as cropland is lost to erosion. Humans must show a new respect for the soil. Many nations have begun to recognize this and take action. In the late 1960s Japan passed a law forbidding construction on cropland.[153] The United States installed a conservation program in 1987 that encouraged farmers to protect the land.[154] Incentives were offered for taking marginal, erodable land out of crop production and turning it into grassland or woods. Poor soil-management practices were penalized by a reduction in farm-program benefits. The program is estimated to reduce soil losses by 460 million tons a year.

Alternatives must be found for vulnerable monocrop fields. Instead of viewing trees as obstacles to machinery, farmers could be informed of the benefits of having trees mixed with crops. Many tropical and subtropical regions have discovered the advantages of agroforestry. Whereas the usual farming procedure has been to clear the ground completely, agroforestry calls for the strategic planting of trees on cropland. These trees increase the productivity of the farm by furnishing organic matter and nitrogen to the soil and providing forage, food, fuel, and protection from wind erosion.

In a number of cases, balanced sustainable production could best be achieved by reverting to time-honored practices. Crop rotation has long been used to keep the soil from being exhausted by the continuous demands of a single crop. Farmers could go a step further in Third World countries by learning (in some cases, returning to) multiple-cropping techniques. Whereas crop rotation simply means varying the crops that are grown in a particular field, multiple cropping involves growing several crops in a field at the same time. This requires far more manual labor than monocropping. But in lands where millions are unable to find meaningful work, labor saving is a low priority compared to this more stable, sustainable use of the soil. Not only does a mixture of plants make better use of the soil, but it also makes better use of sunlight and is less susceptible to devastating disease.[155]

In place of chemical fertilizers, farmers could return to the natural fertilization of recycled organic nutrients. Local waste materials such as manure, compost, wood ash, bone meal, leaves, and egg shells could maintain a stable nutrient content in the soil for a fraction of the cost of artificial fertilizers.

Farmers in Southeast Asia have, for countless generations, used an early form of biotechnology to increase their production.[156] A form of blue-green algae was grown with rice in the paddies. This algae was adept at turning atmospheric nitrogen into a form that the plants could use. Researchers have been seeking out other forms of nitrogen-fixing plants that could grow alongside food crops. A plant called a causarina has shown such promise as an aid to crops that it has been dubbed "the energy tree." Not only does it fix nitrogen for plants, but it grows quickly to provide a ready supply of wood fuel.

Biopesticides are especially crucial to the development of a healthy, stable relationship with the environment. A plant called neem has been found to produce seed kernels that contain a natural insecticide. Carefully researched natural controls on weeds and crop pests could rid the world of a dangerous dependence on long-lived poisons for the protection of crops.

Energy could be recycled from nature rather

than pulled from limited supplies in the ground. Some bacteria are proficient at turning animal wastes into methane gas, a system that solves a waste disposal problem as well as providing energy. China has installed millions of small methane converters to provide affordable, renewable energy for its farmers.[157]

ACCESS TO FOOD

Population control and more careful attention to stable, environmentally sound farming practices may eventually establish an adequate, renewable food supply for the world. But, even so, that would not solve the hunger problem. As has been repeatedly stressed, the terrible famines we have seen in the past decades have not been caused by food shortages. Increased production does not necessarily mean that starving will be reduced. Were we to able to produce ten times as much food tomorrow as we do today, thousands would continue to die from hunger.

The only way to prevent hunger and famine is to see that people have access to food. Two types of barriers prevent people from getting food: physical and economic.

Some physical barriers are beyond the reach of technology. Bad weather, of course, is one of these. Another is warfare. War prevents food from reaching people as surely as if an impenetrable wall were constructed between them. Of the roughly 120 Third World nations, more than a third of them either are or recently were engaged in warfare.[158] An inordinate amount of the world's resources is spent for military purposes. The prevention of war is a subject beyond the scope of this book. But any long-standing effort to eliminate world hunger must work toward peaceful resolution of disputes.

Transportation barriers can be overcome by existing technology. Construction of roads and bridges and the use of trucks, ships, and aircraft can make it possible for enough food to be transported to virtually every part of the earth. Relief efforts often concentrate on improving transportation so farmers can get their products to market and so food can reach drought-stricken villages.

If the primary cause of world hunger is poverty, as many hunger analysts declare, then economic barriers must be the primary focus of concern. Relief organizations must work hard to help local communities develop their economic potential. This may take the form of digging wells, constructing irrigation systems, providing electricity, making loans available for new industries, and other projects.

Just as is true about food production, however, it is one thing to produce economic wealth and quite another to distribute it. Poverty does not result from a lack of wealth in the world. Brazil's per capita income is higher than South Korea's, and yet it has three times as much poverty.[159] From 1968 to 1974 Brazil's economy grew at a robust 10 percent per year. Yet at the end of that time, two-thirds of its population was worse off than ever.[160] Many more people than ever went hungry. China is no wealthier per capita than India. Yet hunger has been virtually wiped out in China while hundreds of millions of Indians do not have an adequate diet.[161] More than 100 million people in nations with moderate-to-above-average standards of living do not get enough

calories to allow them to lead a normal life.[162] The United States, with its relatively affluent standard of living, has not rid itself of poverty or malnutrition. The key factor is not the amount of wealth the country owns but how it is distributed.

Hungry people are poor people who have been cut out of the economic system. They are farmers who have no land, citizens who have no vote, urban dwellers who have no job, women who have no status, children who have no rights. The best way to eliminate hunger is to work for economic justice in the world. Economic injustice can be attacked on several fronts: national government, the international community, and technological development.

On a national scale, Third World governments must resist the temptation to build wealth through industry at the expense of agriculture. Since three-fourths of their populations is involved in agriculture, such policies favor the urban few at the expense of the rural majority. India, while still facing grave hunger problems, has achieved progress through a government program that guarantees a

Girl working in a rice field
in Sichuan Province, China.
Why is it that China,
no wealthier per capita
than India, has virtually
eliminated hunger, whereas
millions of Indians are
malnourished? The answer may lie
in better distribution.

fair and stable price for food.[163] China used economic reform to boost its food production by 50 percent between 1976 and 1984.[164] Other Third World nations must make certain that rural farmers are treated fairly so they have an adequate chance to earn a living.

Second, changes must be made in the way that governments regulate land ownership. Land is a limited, vital resource. Countries that allow abuse of this resource are committing suicide. In recent years, more and more land has fallen into the hands of the wealthy. There are currently four times the number of landless people in Central America as there were in 1960.[165] In Brazil, 2 percent of landowners control 60 percent of the farmland. In Bangladesh, one of the poorest countries in Asia, a third of the rural people own no land.[166] In Africa, nomadic herdsmen are denied the right to roam across lands they have fed off for centuries. This is not merely a Third World problem. In the United States, the majority of the land is owned by a tiny percentage of people. Each year more small farms go out of business, their land taken over by wealthier farm interests. The United States Department of Agriculture estimates that by the year 2000, 4 percent of the farmers will own 60 percent of the arable land in the United States.[167] The loss of land has denied millions of rural people all over the world the means to earn a living.

It has been well documented that people who own a share of the land are more likely to care for it. A study in Iowa showed that tenant farmers lose a third more topsoil than farmers who own their own land.[168] Absentee landlords are more likely to be looking for short-term profit in farming enterprises.

That means planting high-yield, soil-depleting cash crops in place of food crops.

One of the single most effective tools in battling world hunger is land reform. Countries that have instituted serious programs to redistribute land more evenly among the people have shown remarkable declines in hunger. Japan, following World War II, Korea and Taiwan in the 1950s, China in the 1970s, and Nicaragua in the early 1980s (before civil war accelerated) all achieved greater food yields as a result of such programs.[169]

Along with more equitable land reform, democratic reform can reduce world hunger. People who have a voice in their government are less likely to be abused by corrupt and callous leaders. They are less likely to be pushed into the kind of desperation that results in civil war. Further, workers who have a say in the affairs of their country are more likely to be productive than those who are strapped with unfair policies.

On an international scale, Third World nations often face enormous obstacles in trying to compete in world markets. They find themselves pitted against other countries with far greater financial backing, more advanced technology, more determined government support, and better educated labor forces. In order to compete they are pushed into drastic new policies aimed at immediately adopting a way of life that Western industrialized nations were able to develop over the course of a century.

For most, the odds are too heavily stacked against them. Export earnings for the poorest Third World countries are falling. In 1986 the price that Third World countries received for raw commodities was the lowest in history compared to the price of finished goods.[170] Their purchasing power in world markets has been steadily shrinking. Third World countries who tried to make use of Western finances to build up their economies now find themselves crushed under a trillion-dollar debt to those nations. The decline of food production per capita in Latin America can be traced to its mounting debt crisis, which first became serious in the early 1980s.[171]

The international community responded admirably to Africa's cry of anguish in the mid-1980s. But the apparent generosity was somewhat misleading. In the decade prior to the famine, many countries made a handsome profit on the food they sold to African countries. At the same time that its earnings from food sales were climbing in the 1970s, the United States was cutting back its contributions to food aid. The amount given in aid to Africa in 1985 did not begin to match the amount of money that foreign countries took out of Africa.[172]

Nor did it match the billions of tax dollars that Western nations spent to subsidize their own agriculture. Third World countries, unable to match that, lost out in the world grain market. The price they received for wheat on the international market dropped by a third from 1981 to 1986.[173] Africa, once a food-exporting region, has been practically driven out of the agriculture business and now cannot feed its own people.

There is also some question of whether the small amount of foreign aid given to famine-struck countries has been effective in fighting economic injustice. Industrial countries have been providing foreign aid almost exclusively to those governments with whom they are politically allied. Little pressure has been put on those governments to take seriously the task of feeding their people or of maintaining democracy. Foreign aid, therefore, often results in propping up the very types of government that promote injustice and thus allow their people to starve.

When a famine crisis becomes so bad that industrial nations are moved to help regardless of the political alliance of the government, such as in Ethiopia, the aid is only a short-term fix. It keeps people alive temporarily but does little to change the conditions that caused the famine and will cause the next famine.

Hunger experts suggest that rather than distributing morsels of charity during an acute famine, industrial nations should work to bring justice to the trade situation. Unless Third World nations can produce goods to trade internationally, and unless they receive a reasonable price for those goods, there is little hope of preventing repeated massive famine. Among the steps that could be taken by the international community would be a restructuring of debts so that Third World countries are not bled dry by interest payments. Economic and democratic reform must be encouraged.

International groups considering giving aid should remember that grand schemes rarely work. Individual communities face different environmental problems. They depend on different traditions and social customs to lend stability to their communities. Rather than drawing up elaborate plans for fighting hunger, efforts need to be focused on helping communities develop in ways that meet their own needs and desires.

Industrial nations must also exercise restraint in

Bags of sorghum from the
United States being distributed in
Burkina Faso as part of a relief program

consumption. Currently they are using up far more than their share of the world's limited resources. If all humans are to share in the earth's wealth, affluent nations must stop wasting these resources. If the earth is to be in any shape to support all humans on Earth, then the wealthy must cut back on energy consumption and pollution.

Many are opposed to the idea of government intervention in political matters. Western industrialists often favor the idea of free markets. They believe that the law of supply and demand and the incentive of private rewards do a far better job of promoting economic growth than does government meddling. The collapse of the state-controlled governments of Eastern Europe in recent times is cited as proof that government action does more harm than good. This point of view favors the work of private organizations in addressing social needs of the world.

On the other hand, it is argued that the free market responds only to money, not to need. There is something seriously wrong with a free market system that concentrates so much wealth and power in the hands of a few while billions cannot even get enough food to stay alive. The only way to share power effectively is through democracy, and democracy is a characteristic of government, not of the free enterprise system. In addition, land is such a precious asset to society that people cannot be allowed to do whatever they please with it. The privilege of owning land carries with it an obligation to act responsibly. Only democratic governments can enforce that obligation.

The economic redistribution of wealth is primarily a political matter. But science and technology have not been entirely blameless in the widening gap between the wealthy and the poor. The technology of the twentieth century has been largely designed to help the wealthy at the expense of the poor. New technologies have required more money, more equipment, and more expertise than the methods they have replaced. This has often put the new technology out of reach of the poor farmer, and so it has benefited the wealthy.

We have briefly looked at the effect of the Green Revolution on poor farmers in less-developed parts of the world. But technology has been the ally of the wealthy against the poor in industrial countries as well as in Third World countries. In the United States, small farmers have been steadily driven out of business by huge industrial-agricultural companies. Already in the 1980s 1 percent of the farmers collect more than half of the net farm income in the country.[174] One percent of the feedlots in the United States raise 60 percent of the beef cattle.

The legacy of technology is one of widening the gap between rich and poor. The average person in industrial countries now lives a life of greater luxury than at any other time in human history. But this has occurred while famines develop that are more brutal than at any other time in history.

Some have suggested that technology merely replaces small problems with great problems. They advocate returning to simpler ways. Others point out the benefits of technology in increasing standards of living. They believe that a change of priorities is all that is needed. Science and technology should concentrate on ways to improve the standing of the desperately poor.

If technology is to be useful in ending world hunger, then it must stop concentrating blindly on increasing production. Instead, researchers must make "appropriateness" their primary goal. A technology advance is not appropriate if it puts workers out of a job for the sake of increased production. It is not appropriate if it places additional demands or risks on the environment, if it substitutes luxuries for basics, if it destroys the culture that is in place, if it increases dependence on outside experts, or if it carries an expense that favors wealthy farmers over poor.[175]

One way in which technology is being used as an aid to the poor is in hunger forecasting. By measuring the climatic conditions and estimating the yields of farms, scientists are able to predict when severe famine will strike. The world was caught off guard by the terrible African famine of 1983. Emergency food supplies arrived far too late to prevent most of the destruction. In 1988, however, an early warning system alerted relief organizations to another likely famine in Ethiopia.[176] This time, food supplies and a distribution system were in place from the start. By getting an early jump on famines, relief groups can reach people before hunger forces the widespread evacuation of farms and communities that sets the stage for future famines.

CHAPTER 8

A MATTER
OF WILL

On one television channel you can watch tiny human skeletons wasting away from starvation. On another you may see children slipping and slopping through tons of food in a relay race, just for the fun of it. While riding on a luxury ocean liner serving eight sumptuous meals a day, you can sail past shores of people who crave a few scraps of bread.

Do we need any more evidence that hunger is injustice? That it is born of greed and ignorance and a lack of respect for fellow humans, for the gift of food, and for the earth that supplies it?

The injustice of hunger is so firmly entrenched that eliminating it will not be easy. Horrendous famines could devastate our planet before we ever come to grips with the issue.

Solving the hunger problem requires some people to give up a small portion of what they have for the sake of others. On a personal scale, humans are quite capable of doing so. They are willing to sacrifice for a family member, a friend, or a fellow group member. But will they sacrifice for a stranger? And if so, will they sacrifice enough? The track record of humans in this regard has not been encouraging.

Two main issues affect world hunger—how to get enough food and how to distribute it to everyone.

The first problem deals with limits. Science and technology have been able to increase the amount of food that we can get from the environment. Biotechnology and other scientific disciplines offer a number of possibilities for expanding the available food supply even more. Even so, if the world's population continues to grow at a rapid rate, it will eventually surpass the ability of the earth to supply it with food. In order to ensure food for the future, population must be contained.

Many of our current methods of producing food are wasteful, harmful, or dangerous to our environment. As the earth's population puts a greater strain on our resources, these methods will become increasingly worrisome. As good land becomes scarce, we will see that it makes no sense to farm it so intensively that it wears down. As we reach the limits of our food supply, we may find that we will have to cut down on inefficient luxury items in our diet. As chemical levels in the ground and water and carbon emission in the air grow more toxic, we will either cut back on their use or perish.

As we reach the limits, a stable food supply will only be assured if we shift the emphasis from maximum production to sustainable production. We will have to learn how to work with nature, to stop taking more from the environment then we give back to it.

Second, regardless of the food supply, world hunger will never be stopped unless we find ways of getting food into the stomachs of the hungry. Emergency aid to starving people is necessary to keep people alive. But it only postpones the problem for another day, when the problem will be even greater. After awhile, people become numbed to crisis. "Compassion fatigue" sets in as people are asked again and again to contribute to situations that only get worse. If that happens, we have lost all hope of solving the problem.

Massive efforts are needed to help local communities develop their own sustainable production systems. International markets have to be re-examined to find ways that will allow the poor of the world to participate. Democracy and human rights must be stressed at all levels of government.

South Carolina senator Ernest Hollings has said, "The United States has the ability to wipe out hunger almost overnight. We can, we just haven't."[177] He was speaking about hunger in the United States, but he could have been talking about the world. There is no excuse for it. Human beings have eliminated human sacrifice and slavery from the civilized world. We could do the same with another barbaric practice—the practice of allowing millions to starve to death. It is simply a matter of will.

SOURCE NOTES

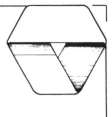

1. Frances Moore Lappé, *World Hunger* (New York: Grove Press, 1986).
2. Roberts L. Stivers, *Hunger, Technology & Limits to Growth* (Minneapolis: Augsburg, 1984).
3. E. J. Kahn, Jr., *Staffs of Life* (Boston: Little, Brown, 1985).
4. William Byron, *The Causes of World Hunger* (New York: Paulist Press, 1982).
5. Nance Lui Fyson, *Feeding the World* (London: Batsford Academic & Educational, 1984).
6. L. R. Brown, "The Grain Drain: The Waning of Food Security," *The Futurist* (August 1989).
7. Ibid.
8. L. R. Brown, "The World Food Crisis," *USA Today* (March 1989).
9. Brown, "The Grain Drain."
10. Brown, "The World Food Crisis."
11. Ibid.
12. Byron, *The Causes of World Hunger*.
13. L. Williamson, "The Ultimate Wildlife Threat," *Outdoor Life* (December 1987).
14. Jack Doyle, *Altered Harvests* (New York: Viking, 1985).
15. Brown, "The Grain Drain."
16. Byron, *The Causes of World Hunger*.

17. S. McCurry, "Africa's Sahel: The Stricken Land," *National Geographic* (August 1987).
18. Brown, "The World Food Crisis."
19. Ibid.
20. McCurry, "Africa's Sahel."
21. Lappé, *World Hunger*.
22. Independent Commission on International Humanitarian Issues, *Famine: A Man-Made Disaster?* (New York: Vintage Books, 1985).
23. Brown, "The World Food Crisis."
24. Ibid.
25. W. S. Ellis, "A Soviet Sea Lies Dying," *National Geographic* (February 1990).
26. Brown, "The World Food Crisis."
27. "Mono Lake to Get Some Water Back," *National Geographic* (February 1990).
28. Brown, "The World Food Crisis."
29. Ed Edwin, *Feast or Famine: Food, Farming & Farm Politics in America* (New York: Charterhouse, 1974).
30. Arthur Simon, *Bread for the World*, rev. ed (New York: Paulist Press, 1984).
31. R. Gore, "Between Monterey Tides," *National Geographic* (February 1990).
32. ICIHI, *Famine: A Man-Made Disaster?*
33. Nigel Calder, *The Green Machines* (New York: Putnam, 1986).
34. Lappé, *World Hunger*.
35. Ellis, "A Soviet Sea Lies Dying."
36. Lappé, *World Hunger*.
37. Ibid.
38. *Time* (September 19, 1988).
39. Doyle, *Altered Harvests*.
40. Brown, "The Grain Drain."
41. Doyle, *Altered Harvests*.
42. M. Davidson, "You Can't Build Peace on Empty Stomachs," *USA Today* (September 1988).
43. Elie Schneour, *The Malnourished Mind* (New York: Doubleday, 1974).
44. Fyson, *Feeding the World*.

45. Ibid.
46. Simon, *Bread for the World.*
47. Schneour, *The Malnourished Mind.*
48. Loretta Schwartz-Nobel, *Starving in the Shadow of Plenty* (New York: Putnam, 1981).
49. Schneour, *The Malnourished Mind.*
50. Schwartz-Nobel, *Starving in the Shadow.*
51. P. Kopvillem, "New Hope for Children," *Macleans* (February 1986).
52. ICIHI, *Famine: A Man-Made Disaster?*
53. Ibid.
54. Ibid.
55. J. Wilde, "Starvation in a Fruitful Land," *Time* (December 5, 1988).
56. J. Greenwald, "Agony on the African Continent," *Time* (February 2, 1988).
57. Ronald J. Sider, *Rich Christians in an Age of Hunger* (Downers Grove, Ill: Inter-Varsity, 1977).
58. Brown, "The Grain Drain."
59. Ibid.
60. Kahn, *Staffs of Life.*
61. Fyson, *Feeding the World.*
62. ICIHI, *Famine: A Man-Made Disaster?*
63. Ibid.
64. Davidson, "You Can't Build Peace."
65. ICIHI, *Famine: A Man-Made Disaster?*
66. Ibid.
67. Simon, *Bread for the World.*
68. ICIHI, *Famine: A Man-Made Disaster?*
69. B. T. Olson, "Two Faces of Malnutrition," *The Lutheran Standard* (March 6, 1979).
70. Lappé, *World Hunger.*
71. Jack Anderson column, February 1990.
72. Byron, *The Causes of World Hunger.*
73. Harold C. Nelson & Irving Kaplan, eds., *Ethiopia: A Country Study* (Washington, D.C.: Foreign Area Studies, 1981).
74. R. Wilson, "Five Years After the Famine," *Christianity Today* (October 6, 1989).

75. Nelson and Kaplan, *Ethiopia*.
76. Ibid.
77. M. Serrill, "Famine," *Time* (December 21, 1987).
78. Myles Harris, *Breakfast in Hell* (New York: Poseidon Press, 1987).
79. Serrill, "Famine."
80. Harris, *Breakfast in Hell*.
81. ICIHI, *Famine: A Man-Made Disaster?*
82. Harris, *Breakfast in Hell*.
83. Wilde, "Starvation in a Fruitful Land."
84. Harris, *Breakfast in Hell*.
85. M. Serrill, "Twin Plagues of War & Famine," *Time* (March 28, 1988).
86. Edwin, *Feast or Famine?*
87. Ibid.
88. Ibid.
89. Ibid.
90. Kahn, *Staffs of Life*.
91. Ibid.
92. Ibid.
93. Ibid.
94. Ibid.
95. Fyson, *Feeding the World*.
96. Douglas Bishop, *Crop Science & Food Production* (New York: McGraw-Hill, 1983).
97. Paul Ehrlich, *The Population Bomb* (River City, Mass.: River City Press, 1971).
98. Simon, *Bread for the World*.
99. Ibid.
100. Calder, *The Green Machines*.
101. Brown, "The World Food Crisis."
102. Ibid.
103. ICIHI, *Famine: A Man-Made Disaster?*
104. Bishop, *Crop Science & Food Production*.
105. Ibid.
106. Simon, *Bread for the World*.
107. Lappé, *World Hunger*.
108. Bishop, *Crop Science & Food Production*.
109. Ibid.
110. Calder, *The Green Machines*.

111. Bishop, *Crop Science & Food Production*.
112. Ibid.
113. Ibid.
114. Kahn, *Staffs of Life*.
115. Lappé, *World Hunger*.
116. Kahn, *Staffs of Life*.
117. Bishop, *Crop Science & Food Production*.
118. Ibid.
119. Fyson, *Feeding the World*.
120. Ibid.
121. Simon, *Bread for the World*.
122. Lappé, *World Hunger*.
123. Simon, *Bread for the World*.
124. Ibid.
125. Kahn, *Staffs of Life*.
126. Calder, *The Green Machines*.
127. Kahn, *Staffs of Life*.
128. P. Abelson, "World Food Research," *Science* (April 14, 1989).
129. Calder, *The Green Machines*.
130. Elizabeth Antebi & David Fishlock, *Biotechnologies: Strategies for Life* (Cambridge, Mass.: MIT Press, 1986).
131. Doyle, *Altered Harvests*.
132. Ibid.
133. Ibid.
134. Antebi & Fishlock, *Biotechnologies*.
135. Calder, *The Green Machines*.
136. Antebi & Fishlock, *Biotechnologies*.
137. Ibid.
138. Kahn, *Staffs of Life*.
139. E. M. DuPuis & C. C. Geisler, "Biotechnology and the Small Farmer," *Bioscience* (June 1988).
140. Ibid.
141. D. Wyss, "A Furious Battle Over Milk," *Time* (May 29, 1989).
142. Ibid.
143. "Medical Society Says BGH Safe," Associated Press article (January 24, 1990).
144. Wyss, "A Furious Battle Over Milk."

145. DuPuis & Geisler, "Biotechnology and the Small Farmer."
146. Michael Bayles, *Morality & Population Policy* (University of Alabama Press, 1980).
147. Simon, *Bread for the World*.
148. Louis L. Knowles, *A Guide to World Hunger Organizations* (Seeds/Alternatives, 1984).
149. Ibid.
150. Jacquelyn Kasun, *War on Population* (San Francisco: Ignatius Press, 1988).
151. Doyle, *Altered Harvests*.
152. Kahn, *Staffs of Life*.
153. Brown, "The Grain Drain."
154. Ibid.
155. Ibid.
156. Calder, *The Green Machines*.
157. Ibid.
158. Kopvillem, "New Hope for Children."
159. Byron, *Causes of World Hunger*.
160. Sider, *Rich Christians*.
161. Davidson, "You Can't Build Peace."
162. J. W. Helmuth, "World Hunger Amidst Plenty," *USA Today* (March 1989).
163. Fyson, *Feeding the World*.
164. Helmuth, "World Hunger Amidst Plenty."
165. Lappé, *World Hunger*.
166. Fyson, *Feeding the World*.
167. Doyle, *Altered Harvests*.
168. Lappé, *World Hunger*.
169. Ibid.
170. Ibid.
171. Simon, *Bread for the World*.
172. Helmuth, "World Hunger Amidst Plenty."
173. Calder, *The Green Machines*.
174. ICIHI, *Famine: A Man-Made Disaster?*
175. DuPuis & Geisler, "Biotechnology and the Small Farmer."
176. ICIHI, *Famine: A Man-Made Disaster?*
177. Simon, *Bread for the World*.

BIBLIOGRAPHY

Books

Antebi, Elizabeth and David Fishlock. *Biotechnologies: Strategies for Life.* Cambridge, Mass.: MIT Press, 1986.

Bishop, Douglas. *Crop Science and Food Production.* New York: McGraw-Hill, 1983.

Byron, William. *The Causes of World Hunger.* New York: Paulist Press, 1982.

Calder, Nigel. *The Green Machines.* New York: Putnam's, 1986.

Doyle, Jack. *Altered Harvests.* New York: Viking, 1985.

Edwin, Ed. *Feast or Famine: Food, Farming and Farm Politics in America.* New York: Charterhouse, 1974.

Ehrlich, Paul. *The Population Bomb.* River City, Mass.: River City Press, 1971.

Fyson, Nance Lui. *Feeding the World.* London: Batsford Academic & Educational, 1984.

Harris, Myles. *Breakfast in Hell*. New York: Poseidon Press, 1987.

Independent Commission on International Humanitarian Issues. *Famine: A Man-Made Disaster?* New York: Vintage Books, 1985.

Kahn, E. J., Jr. *Staffs of Life*. Boston: Little, Brown, 1985.

Knowles, Louis L. *A Guide to World Hunger Organizations*. Seeds/Alternatives, 1984.

Lappé, Frances Moore. *World Hunger*. New York: Grove Press, 1986.

Nelson, Harold C. & Irving Kaplan, eds. *Ethiopia: A Country Study*. Washington, D.C.: Foreign Area Studies, 1981.

Schneour, Elie. *The Malnourished Mind*. New York: Doubleday, 1974.

Schwartz-Nobel, Loretta. *Starving in the Shadow of Plenty*. New York: Putnam, 1981.

Sider, Ronald J. *Rich Christians in an Age of Hunger*. Downers Grove, Ill.: Inter-Varsity, 1977.

Simon, Arthur. *Bread for the World*. Rev. ed. New York: Paulist Press, 1984.

Stivers, Robert L. *Hunger, Technology & Limits to Growth.* Minneapolis: Augsburg, 1984.

INDEX

ABOUT THE AUTHOR

Nathan Aaseng is the author of over seventy books for children and adults on such diverse subjects as sports, inventors, medicine, and zoology. He has also worked as a research microbiologist. Mr. Aaseng holds a bachelor's degree in English and biology from Luther College. He lives with his wife and four children in Eau Claire, Wisconsin.